PRAISE FOR
Driving Excellence

"In this book, Steve Sanghi and Michael Jones share with us the schematic diagram they created to transform and grow Microchip into the Cinderella story of the semiconductor industry. The *Aggregate System* detailed in this book is a proven, holistic methodology for building and maintaining a great company in any industry!"

> **Roy Vallee**
> Chairman and CEO,
> Avnet, Inc.

"Steve and Michael, as leaders of a fast growing successful technology company, have shown the passion and commitment to write down their leadership philosophy in detail. It is a well organized compendium of immense common sense. Their values based, walk-the-talk approach recognizes the fast changing environment we live in. It shows the importance of aggregating and integrating knowledge and experience on a continuous basis. Finally, it demonstrates the significance of creating a culture that reinforces those values and takes pride in thriving on the complexity."

> **John E. Abele**
> Founder and Director,
> Boston Scientific Corporation

"In this book, Steve and Michael reveal the cultural secrets of Microchip Technology, one of Arizona High Tech's brightest stars. The *Aggregate System* is a powerful blend of strategic formula, exceptional culture and human systems combined into a complete self-perpetuating system to produce exceptional performance. Anyone interested in improving the performance of his or her company should read this book."

> **Jerry Colangelo**
> Chairman and CEO,
> Phoenix Suns

"This is not another 'silver bullet' piece of academic advice on how to do a 'quick fix' to some imaginary business. *Driving Excellence* is a serious and detailed insight into how a real CEO, Steve Sanghi, has transformed a real company, Microchip, into a multibillion dollar world-class enterprise. Anyone interested in understanding the realities of implementing and sustaining an enterprise-wide constant improvement plan should read this book."

Dean Kamen
Founder and President,
DEKA Research and Development
Corporation; Inventor of Segway HT;
Science Hall of Fame Inductee

"Managing organizational complexities is a task that befuddles all leaders in all sectors. Michael and Steve in *Driving Excellence* have found a way to address complexity as they outline through their experience the mechanisms by which one can bring about organizational success. Complexity is always the issue and it is often the case that people move to oversimplify. Michael and Steve do the opposite. They provide a mechanism to embrace complexity and to move forward across all of the elements necessary to bring about organizational improvement and organizational success in a way that is straightforward and easily understandable across multiple sectors. I believe that *Driving Excellence* offers much for managers and CEOs in the public, private, and hybrid organizational sectors. Therefore, I urge everyone to give it very careful consideration."

Michael M. Crow
President,
Arizona State University

"*Driving Excellence* is the first book to deal with the integration of all the core elements that are essential to running a business. It should be required reading for all executives and venture firms looking to boost return on invested capital and add some consistency to their growth. High praise is due to Michael Jones and Steve Sanghi for developing a blueprint that works in the real world."

Ed Sperling
Editor in Chief,
Electronic News

"In most businesses today, the pace is accelerating, the complexity increasing, and the competitive pressures growing. How do you, as an organization, survive and more importantly, strive to lead? *Driving Excellence* is a pragmatic answer to this question from two people (Steve Sanghi and Michael Jones) who have first hand and personal experience over years of making it happen. Their approach pulls together many methods in a holistic system. It drives results by focusing on the key aspects that drive individuals to function at their full potential in their role in the organisation. This will be a constant reference on my desk."

Andrew Sukawaty
CEO,
Inmarsat Plc

"*Driving Excellence* presents a systems approach to the development of a corporate culture that will provide continuous improvement for a business and, at the same time, promote employee job satisfaction. The principles are expressed very clearly, make sense and are easy to understand, the frequent use of examples adds to the clarity of the text. As a university president for 14 years, I can state that the *Aggregate System* described in this book can be applied to the administration of a university just as well as that of a for-profit corporation. The success of Microchip as a result of the application of the *Aggregate System*, adds a great deal of credibility to this work. I highly recommend the text for corporate executives and those having management aspirations."

James E.A. John, PhD
Former President,
Kettering University

"The *Aggregate System*, a.k.a. the 'ultimate system,' illustrates the transformational roadmap to corporate excellence, through the methodology of the continuous rate of improvement by keeping the culture and incentive in alignment. This system is a comprehensive masterpiece, which fosters innovation, execution, improvement and incentive through total organizational empowerment. Sanghi and Jones deserve a standing ovation for this 'breakthrough' treatise on leadership, management, empowerment, culture as the foundation to continuously improving performance."

Ed Zito
President and CEO,
Alliance Bank of Arizona

"This book provides a nicely-developed framework to understand organizational effectiveness and performance, drawing upon Steve's managerial skills, perfected in his significant turnaround performance at Microchip; importantly, the reader benefits from insight and experience about building an organizational culture productive to performance and competitiveness."

Steven Stralser, PhD
Author of *MBA in a Day*; Clinical Professor and Managing Director, Global Entrepreneurship Center at Thunderbird: The Garvin School of International Management

"The *Aggregate System* outlined in this book provides a practical and comprehensive methodology for transforming good organizations into great ones. *Driving Excellence* presents sound, structured guidance for any management team committed to positive change."

Steve Barber
CEO,
Xyratex Ltd

"What I like most about *Driving Excellence*, is its focus on the values of the organization as the foundation for the rest of the system. It's great to see the emphasis given to the development of the employee assets to create self-perpetuating improvement that drives the competitiveness of the total organization in a world of constant change. Great job Steve and Michael. Thanks for sharing your leanings!"

Ernest Sampias
Former CFO,
McData Systems, Inc.

Driving Excellence

Driving Excellence

How the *Aggregate System*
Turned Microchip Technology From
a Failing Company to a Market Leader

Michael J. Jones
Steve Sanghi

WILEY

John Wiley & Sons, Inc.

Published by John Wiley & Sons, Inc., Hoboken, New Jersey
Published simultaneously in Canada

Figures by Michael J. Jones

For general information on our other products and services or for technical support, please contact our Customer Care Department within the United States at (800) 762-2974, outside the United States at (317) 572-3993 or fax (317) 572-4002.

Wiley also publishes its books in a variety of electronic formats. Some content that appears in print may not be available in electronic books. For more information about Wiley products, visit our web site at www.wiley.com.

Write to Michael J. Jones at mikejjones@cox.net or Steve Sanghi at Steve.Sanghi@Microchip.com

Library of Congress Cataloging-in-Publication Data:

Sanghi, Steve, 1955–
    Driving excellence : how the aggregate system turned Microchip Technology from a failing company to a market leader / Steve Sanghi, Michael J. Jones.
        p. cm.
    Includes index.
    ISBN-13: 978-0-471-78484-5 (cloth)
    ISBN-10: 0-471-78484-2 (cloth)
    1. Microchip Technology, Inc.—Management. 2. Semiconductor industry—United States—Management. 3. Organizational effectiveness. 4. Corporate culture. 5. Industrial management. I. Jones, Michael J., 1958– II. Title.
    HD9696.S44M537   2006
    338.7'6213950973—dc22

                                                                                    2005029728

Printed in the United States of America

20 19 18 17 16 15 14 13 12

I dedicate this book and the rest of my life to my wife, Andrea, whose love and assistance supported this undertaking.

MJJ

I dedicate this book to my wife, Maria; to my two children, Christie and Jason; and to Microchip Technology Inc.'s 3,900 employees, whose hard work, perseverance, and results made me worthy of this authorship.

SS

Contents

Foreword

As a former consultant to Microchip Technology and a current board member, I have observed firsthand how taking a systems approach has turned an average company into the highest-performing semiconductor company in the world. In my 30 years' experience in the technology industry, I have never seen a company stride to its destiny so confidently and with so few missteps as has Microchip.

Today, Microchip has a strong culture, an ingenious rewards system, a profound knowledge of the industry, a systematic approach capable of handling business-environment complexities, and the ability to attain peak performance from everyone associated with the company. One secret to this success has been Microchip's great fortune in having Steve Sanghi as its leader. I have had the pleasure to work with Steve since he was one of Intel's most promising young stars, and I was delighted, but not surprised, to see Microchip blossom and thrive under his intelligent, far-seeing, and selfless direction. Michael Jones was instrumental in guiding Microchip toward the set of core values on which its success is based. He spent the full measure of his time and energy at Microchip ensuring that every aspect of the company's behavior is in sync with these principles.

A complaint often heard about business schools is that they tend to produce students heavy on theory but poorly equipped to deal with unquantifiable issues that are the "stuff of management." This book is about the stuff of management. It guides the reader through Microchip's process of developing its systems approach. I am confident that *Driving Excellence* will provide a roadmap for anyone interested in turning his or her company into a juggernaut.

L. B. Day
President
L. B. Day & Company Inc.

Preface

TODAY, MICROCHIP TECHNOLOGY, INC., a worldwide semiconductor company, continues to maintain its track record of outstanding performance. However, this is a far cry from its humble and tenuous beginnings. In 1990, the future of Microchip appeared bleak. It was losing money, sales were dropping, the product portfolio was unimpressive, quality problems were abundant, its technology was archaic, factories were underperforming, and employee job satisfaction was low.

Steve Sanghi was appointed president of Microchip, and was assigned to rapidly turn the enterprise into a success story. Steve, as well as Michael Jones, then the manager of Organizational Development, pondered the various scenarios facing the ailing company. Several consultants had proposed ways to improve Microchip. One suggested that Microchip focus on cycle time reduction to liberate cash. Another claimed quality improvements should be the priority. Others recommended everything from implementing statistical process control to closing the factories and outsourcing manufacturing. Essentially, each consultant said that his or her particular field of expertise would lift Microchip out of trouble.

Steve and Michael appreciated the validity of each consultant's proposal. For the past 50 years, educators, researchers, authors, and consultants have been merchandising their specific piece of expertise as the panacea for improving businesses. However, these piecemeal approaches were insufficient to turn around Microchip's performance and lead it into the top echelon of semiconductor companies. Instead, Microchip needed an approach or system that efficiently and continuously improved all aspects of the enterprise and involved each employee in this quest; only then could the company maximize its rate of improvement. This inspired Steve and Michael to design the *Aggregate System*, outlined in this book.

The *Aggregate System* is a clear and comprehensive roadmap for implementing a self-perpetuating system to guide management and employees in this process. The *Aggregate System* shows you how to attain extraordinary results from the average employee in order to maximize the firm's rate of improvement.

The intensely competitive global marketplace compels companies to optimize their rate of improvement. The marketplace is unforgiving of firms that improve too slowly. Over the long haul, the companies that can continuously improve all aspects of the enterprise will prosper.

Companies may excel in a given area such as R&D, product development, manufacturing, marketing, sales, customer service, technical support, quality, cycle times, planning, inventory management, or maintaining low-cost structures. Others may excel at forming winning strategies, making advantageous decisions, adapting to changing market conditions, or raising capital. Another company's forte may lie in its ability to lead, manage, motivate, retain, and develop a talented workforce.

The real question is which of the attributes cited best position firms to flourish in today's and tomorrow's dynamic and perplexing marketplace? The answer is that companies that sustain a superior rate of improvement in all aspects of their business will be the ones who do well. To reach this goal, companies must be able to continuously improve all aspects of the business in a balanced fashion, not just one element or attribute of the enterprise.

The *Aggregate System* provides a process for constructing the enterprise, sets out a complete system to consciously design an exceptional culture, and demonstrates a highly effective management approach. These three aspects, when combined, yield astonishing results.

Acknowledgments

ABOVE ALL I WISH to acknowledge Steve Sanghi, Microchip Technology's CEO and chairman of the board of directors. Much of my professional success is a direct result of Steve's support, mentoring, and leadership.

I extend my gratitude to the Microchip team. The executives, managers, supervisors, and employees are good and dedicated individuals. The magic of Microchip has always been its people. Microchip's strength stems from thousands of individuals facing and overcoming countless challenges. I would like to acknowledge my former staff at Microchip for their pursuit of excellence.

My wife, Andrea, has played a large role in the writing of this book. She has participated in every step of the process. I value her advice and appreciate her assistance.

MJJ

I WISH TO ACKNOWLEDGE the whole Microchip team, including my staff, from whom I continue to learn every day. The magic of Microchip lies in the dedication of our 3,900 employees, who are our most valuable assets.

I extend my gratitude to Michael Jones, who has been the inspiration behind writing this book and who has documented the highly successful system and culture that we architected at Microchip. I also thank Michael for his advice and support during his 14 years at Microchip. I would like to acknowledge Microchip's board of directors, whose leadership, guidance, and support have been critical to Microchip's success. My special thanks go to Albert Hugo-Martinez, the longest-running board member. His support over the years has been invaluable. I'd also like to thank L. B. Day, who has given me advice and support for over 25 years.

Finally, my wife Maria, and my two children, Christie and Jason, have made a significant sacrifice in their lives, always yielding to the needs of Microchip.

SS

Section One

The Microchip Story— Applying the Aggregate System

Microchip: Before and After

MICROCHIP TECHNOLOGY INCORPORATED, established in April 1989, has its corporate offices in Chandler, Arizona. Microchip, a leading provider of microcontroller and analog semiconductors, focuses on the global embedded control marketplace. Its product line includes PICmicro® microcontrollers (MCUs); an extensive portfolio of analog/interface products; high-endurance Serial EEPROMs; microID® RFID tags; KEELOQ® security devices; and the dsPIC® family of Digital Signal Controllers. Microchip has manufacturing facilities in the United States and Thailand, has sales offices throughout the world, and employs over 3,900 people. The company designs, develops, and manufactures the vast majority of its products.

Humble Beginnings

For many years Microchip's outstanding performance has kept it in the top echelon of semiconductor companies. However, this is a far cry from its tumultuous beginnings. Figure 1.1 provides an insight into the status of Microchip in 1990. Sales were flat to dropping. The disc drive industry generated more than 60% of sales, and a single customer accounted for more than 25% of the business. Both of these factors made Microchip vulnerable to sudden and deep swings in sales. The company was losing $2.5 million

3

Sales	Finance	Manufacturing	Products and Technology
▪ Sales flat to dropping	▪ Losing $2.5 million per quarter	▪ Pathetic yields	▪ Most products and technology many years old
▪ Majority of sales on commodity EPROM products	▪ Heavy negative cash flow	▪ Poor delivery performance	▪ No significant new technology efforts
▪ Sales network built around commodity EPROM products	▪ Less than 6 months of cash at burn rate	▪ Lots of quality issues	▪ Majority of research and development (R&D) going into commodity EPROM products
▪ Gross margin of commodity EPROM products minus 25%	▪ Bank credit line fully tapped	▪ Factory too large for business, yet too inefficient to meet demand	
▪ Largest customer represents over 25% of sales	▪ In violation of bank covenants		▪ Three different programs for EEPROM technology
▪ Disc drive industry represents over 60% of sales	▪ Expenses too high		

Result: Microchip up for sale/liquidation

FIGURE 1.1: Status of Microchip in 1990

per quarter, had less than six months of cash, had exhausted its bank credit lines, and expenses were out of control.

The product portfolio was mediocre and relied heavily on commodity EPROM products. Commodity EPROM products are often compared to jelly beans. They are memory chips that have no inherent defendability. It's easy to switch from one supplier to another. Therefore, price is everything. If your competitors are selling the same memory chips for less, customers will purchase the product from one of them.

Microchip was losing so much money, and the business situation was so bleak, that the company had starved its research and development (R&D) efforts to preserve capital. Moreover, the majority of R&D was still going into commodity EPROM products rather than into new technologies that could provide a higher-margin, more-defendable product line.

Exacerbating Microchip's woes, the manufacturing operation was underperforming. Quality issues ran rampant. The factory was too large for the level of the business, but too inefficient to meet demand. This meant that factory yields (i.e., number of good product produced versus the total product the company attempted to produce) were so low that Microchip couldn't meet its meager demand. Therefore, Microchip had to start production of considerably more product than it actually required because such a large portion was scrapped during the manufacturing process.

In 1990, before we implemented the *Aggregate System* to change Microchip's culture and performance, we conducted anonymous surveys of all U.S. Microchip employees to gauge their perceptions. The results clearly indicated that the employees disdained Microchip's highly rules-based culture, disliked and distrusted management, and had low job satisfaction. We asked the employees how often (i.e., what percentage of the time) Microchip practiced each of the values we were going to install as part of Microchip's new culture. The results were eye opening. Employees stated that under the company's old culture, management, policies and systems, customer service, quality, continuous improvement, employee empowerment, cycle times, profits, communication, and ethics were not practiced or seen as important. In general, the employees did not like the managers, systems, and policies that governed them and the business.

Microchip's overall condition was so grim that the venture capital investors had the company up for sale. They had accepted an offer from Winbond Electronics Corporation of Taiwan for a mere $15 million. Then, in May 1990, the Taiwanese stock market had a setback and Winbond backed out of the deal. In response, Microchip had to look inward to overcome its difficulties. The *Aggregate System* was implemented to provide the foundation for Microchip's transformation. At that time we understood many of the key elements of the system. The system continued to evolve and gain refinement over the years.

Transformation

Microchip needed to *reinvent* itself. This required an immediate and total transformation. The question facing the company was how to reinvent itself in the presence of so many impediments to success. Microchip didn't have great products, it wasn't making money, the operation was shackled by poor execution, and employee job satisfaction was understandably dismal. There was trouble on all fronts. Therefore, we focused on the *foundational strengths to success*: the input factors that lead to success. These input factors are things such as strong workplace values, leadership, customer service, quality workmanship, employee empowerment, ingenuity, perseverance, problem solving, teamwork, adaptability, organization, communication, planning, a true hunger to improve, and so on. We needed to develop an approach (*Aggregate System*) to foster the proliferation of these input factors throughout the enterprise. We began Microchip's turnaround by empowering employees to improve every aspect of the enterprise and by rapidly applying these foundational strengths:

- Inspiring leadership
- A drive to continuously improve every aspect of the enterprise and ourselves
- A total, or aggregate, system for constructing the enterprise, consciously designing an exceptional culture built on strong workplace values (such as serving the customer, producing quality products, reducing costs, innovation, teamwork, and open communication) and practicing a highly effective management approach
- A vision and a roadmap to success outlined in our strategic formula (i.e., the company's vision, mission, strategies, business plans, and profit and loss [P&L]/balance sheet models)
- Outstanding executives and managers with great functional expertise despite being beaten down as a result of working within a highly rules-based, ego-driven, political, nonteamwork culture
- A belief in the capabilities of our employees if we could construct systems and a culture that would unleash their full potential by empowering them to consistently improve their area of responsibility
- In-depth management and organizational development expertise

Formation of the *Aggregate System*

During this period, several consultants proposed ways to improve Microchip. One suggested that Microchip focus on cycle time reduction to liberate cash. Another claimed quality improvement should be the priority.

Others recommended everything from implementing statistical process control to closing the factories and outsourcing manufacturing. Essentially, each consultant said that his or her particular field of expertise would lift Microchip out of its troubles.

We appreciated the validity of each consultant's proposal. For the past 50 years, educators, researchers, authors, and consultants have been promoting their specific area of expertise as the way to improve businesses. However, these piecemeal approaches were insufficient to turn around Microchip's performance and lead it into the top echelon of semiconductor companies. Instead, Microchip needed an approach and a system that *efficiently and continuously improved all aspects of the enterprise and involved each employee in this quest; only then could the company maximize its rate of improvement.* This inspired us to design the *Aggregate System*.

The *Aggregate System*, outlined in this book, was utilized to establish Microchip's culture of uniting employees through shared workplace values and to guide employees' strategies, decisions, actions, and job performance. The enterprise was consciously designed to achieve Microchip's strategic formula (i.e., the company's vision, mission, strategies, business plans, and P&L/balance sheet models). Microchip built the company around a set of core values that led the firm to attain its strategic formula. The company's policies, management practices, and the human systems that influence employees were aligned and integrated to Microchip's values. These human systems encompass how the company organizes, staffs, communicates, assesses, recognizes, compensates, develops, and advances individuals. The leaders served as a role model of Microchip's values through their decisions and actions. Eventually, the *Aggregate System* became self-perpetuating, with each element of Microchip aligning and integrating in unison, maintaining excellence.

Microchip's culture is now characterized by a relentless striving for continuous improvement, employee empowerment and involvement, teamwork, honest and free-flowing communication, problem solving, innovation, merit, frugality, systems thinking, continuous learning, and a results orientation in pursuit of the success of the customers, shareholders, and employees. Microchip possesses each of the elements that exemplify a thriving *Aggregate System*, outlined in Chapter 3. Though this book is dedicated to describing the *Aggregate System* approach, the reader should not assume that this is the primary reason for Microchip's success. Outstanding executives, managers, and employees will always remain the cornerstone of its success. Countless individuals striving to improve operations to better serve the customer have propelled Microchip to prominence. The *Aggregate System* has provided an environment where the employees realize their potential. We think this should be the goal of any great system.

Microchip's Prosperity

Microchip's transformation was successful. In 1993, Microchip conducted its initial public offering (IPO). Microchip was honored by *Fortune* magazine as the best performing IPO of 1993, with a first-year stock price appreciation of 500% and over $1 billion in market capitalization. Figure 1.2 outlines the status of Microchip in 2005. Sales continue to be robust. The majority of the sales are on strategic, high-margin products. The customer base exceeds 46,000, with the largest customer representing only 3% of Microchip's sales. Four of the top ten global distributors sell Microchip products. Sales are nicely balanced among the United States, Europe, and Asia. Microchip sells products to a diverse application and customer base.

For many years, Microchip's financial performance has been outstanding compared to other companies in the semiconductor industry. It is considered to be one of the most profitable (by percentage of revenue) semiconductor companies in the world. Moreover, Microchip has experienced 60 quarters of profitability and has the best financial performance among its specific peer companies. Revenue in fiscal year 2005 was $847 million (Figure 1.3 shows revenue growth over time). Microchip's pro forma gross margin was 57.14%. As shown in Figure 1.4, Microchip's fiscal year 2005 pro forma operating margin was 33%, and its ongoing profitability is illustrated in its solid earnings-per-share track record.

Since 1998, Microchip's market capitalization has increased from approximately $89 million to $5.3 billion (as of March 31, 2005). Microchip's long-term stock appreciation has been impressive. As of February 14, 2005, the stock price has appreciated more than 4,800%, splitting seven

Sales	**Finance**	**Manufacturing**	**Products and Technology**
• Sales growing rapidly	• 60 consecutive quarters of profitability	• World-class manufacturing	• State-of-the-art technology
• Majority of sales on strategic high-margin products	• Best financial performance among peers	• Excellent delivery performance	• Many highly successful new product introductions
• Sales network built around proprietary products	• 33% operating margin	• Excellent quality	• R&D focused on microcontrollers, DSC, and analog products
• Largest customer is only 3% of sales	• Market capitalization in excess of $5.3 billion	• Converted to 8" wafer sizes	• PIC microcontroller: most popular architecture in the world
• Four out of the top 10 global distributors sell Microchip's products	• Expenses in line with P&L model	• High-yield plants in Arizona and Oregon	• Multiple product lines and extensive product portfolio
• Sales balanced among U.S., Europe, and Asia	• Strong cash generation	• Assembly and test plant in Thailand	
• Sell product to a diverse application and customer base	• Strong balance sheet		
• Over 46,000 customers	• Now paying stock dividend	**Result:** Microchip the top-performing IPO of 1993; 4,800% stock price growth since IPO	

FIGURE 1.2: Status of Microchip in 2005

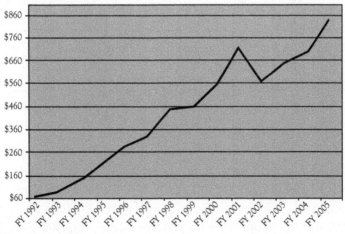

Source: Microchip Technology

FIGURE 1.3: Microchip's Fiscal Year Net Sales (*Millions of Dollars*)

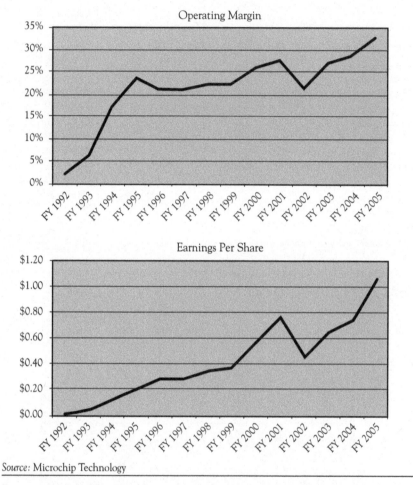

Source: Microchip Technology

Figure 1.4: Microchip's Fiscal Pro Forma Operating Margin and Earnings Per Share

times since the IPO in 1993. As mentioned, Microchip was honored as the top IPO by *Fortune* magazine that year. In 1993, *Fortune* magazine wrote, "The best performing IPO of this year's crop, Microchip Technology can wear the growth stock hat with panache." Figure 1.5 shows that over the past 12 years Microchip's stock outperformed Intel, the Dow Jones Industrial Average, and NASDAQ. Over the past 12 years, Microchip has also had the top performing stock in the semiconductor industry. In fact, during this time period Microchip's stock performance has handily outperformed the 11 "Good to Great" companies Jim Collins cited in his book *Good to Great*. This is a testament to Microchip's stellar stock performance.

Microchip's manufacturing operation is world class. Its yields are excellent and it performs to the highest standards. Its products are built with state-of-the-art technologies, and its product portfolio is extensive. Microchip's PICmicro® microcontroller architecture is the most popular in the world. Figure 1.6 illustrates the increasing appeal of Microchip products. In 1990, Microchip was ranked 20th in global 8-bit microcontroller market share (in units); by 2002 it had jumped to number one, where it remains today. With its extensive portfolio of analog/interface products, PICmicro® microcontrollers (MCUs), high-endurance Serial EEPROMs; microID® RFID tags; KEELOQ® security devices; and the dsPIC® family of Digital

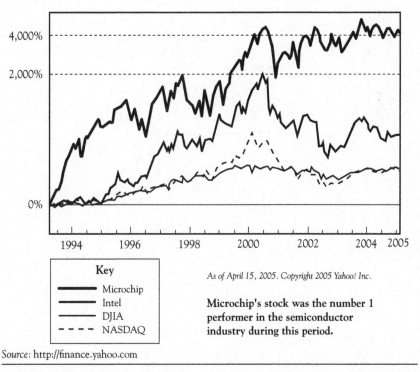

As of April 15, 2005. Copyright 2005 Yahoo! Inc.

Microchip's stock was the number 1 performer in the semiconductor industry during this period.

Source: http://finance.yahoo.com

FIGURE 1.5: Microchip's Stock Performance as Compared to Intel, DJIA, and NASDAQ

No.	1990 Rank	1991-92 Rank	1993 Rank	1994 Rank	1995-96 Rank	1997-01 Rank	2002 Rank	2003 Rank
1	Motorola	Motorola	Motorola	Motorola	Motorola	Motorola	*Microchip* →	*Microchip*
2	Mitsubishi	Mitsubishi	Mitsubishi	Mitsubishi	Mitsubishi	*Microchip*	Motorola	Motorola
3	NEC	Intel	NEC	NEC	SGS	ST-Micro	ST-Micro	Renesas
4	Intel	NEC	Hitachi	Philips	NEC	NEC	NEC	ST-Micro
5	Hitachi	Philips	Philips	Intel	*Microchip*	Philips	Atmel	NEC
6	Philips	Hitachi	Intel	*Microchip*	Philips	Atmel	Sunplus	Atmel
7	Matsushita	Matsushita	SGS	Zilog	Zilog	Hitachi	Hitachi	Sunplus
8	National	SGS	*Microchip*	SGS	Hitachi	Toshiba	Fujitsu	Fujitsu
9	Siemens	National	Matsushita	Matsushita	Fujitsu	Samsung	Philips	Philips
10	TI	TI	Toshiba	Hitachi	Intel	Elan	Toshiba	Toshiba
11	Sharp	Zilog	National	Toshiba	Siemens	Zilog	Mitsubishi	Holtek
12	Oki	Toshiba	Zilog	National	Toshiba	Matsushita	Samsung	Samsung
13	Toshiba	Siemens	TI	TI	Matsushita	Infineon	Elan	Sanyo
14	SGS	*Microchip*	Siemens	Ricoh	TI	Fujitsu	Winbond	Winbond
15	Zilog	Sharp	Sharp	Fujitsu	National	Mitsubishi	Zilog	Infineon
16	Matra MHS	Sanyo	Oki	Siemens	Temic	Sanyo	Sanyo	Matsushita
17	Sony	Matra MHS	Sony	Sharp	Sanyo	Winbond	Matsushita	Sony
18	Fujitsu	Sony	Sanyo	Oki	Ricoh	National	Infineon	Zilog
19	AMD	Oki	Fujitsu	Sony	Oki	Sony	Holtek	National
20	*Microchip*	Fujitsu	AMD	Temic	Sharp	Holtek	National	Elan

Source: Microchip Technology. Based on unit shipment 1990–2003. Dataquest, July 2004

FIGURE 1.6: Worldwide 8-Bit Microcontroller Market Share

Signal Controllers, Microchip maintains a broad product offering to serve its customers and provide financial stability.

Effectiveness of Microchip's Culture

Microchip takes its culture seriously and seeks its employees' input. The company periodically surveys employees to gain insight into the health of the company's culture, the percentage of time the company's values are practiced, the employees' perception of management, and their job satisfaction. When the findings suggest that issues are present, corrective actions are implemented.

The entire U.S. Microchip workforce participates anonymously in these assessments. Figure 1.7 shows the results of Microchip's 2004 assess-

Values	Mean	Mode
▪ Customers Are Our Focus	86%	90%
▪ Quality Comes First	86%	90%
▪ Continuous Improvement Is Essential	83%	90%
▪ Employees Are Our Greatest Strength	77%	90%
▪ Products and Technology Are Our Foundation	86%	90%
▪ Total Cycle Times Are Competitive	85%	90%
▪ Safety Is Never Compromised	89%	100%
▪ Profits and Growth Provide for Everything We Do	89%	100%
▪ Communication Is Vital	86%	90%
▪ Suppliers and Distributors Are Our Partners	82%	90%
▪ Professional Ethics Are Practiced	85%	90%

Note: *Mean score is the average.*
Mode score is the most frequent score given

Source: Microchip Technology's 2004 Survey of U.S. Employees

FIGURE 1.7: Percentage of Time Microchip Practices Its Guiding Values (as Rated by Entire U.S.-Based Employee Population)

Average for U.S. workers: 50%

Microchip's High and Good scores combined: 84%

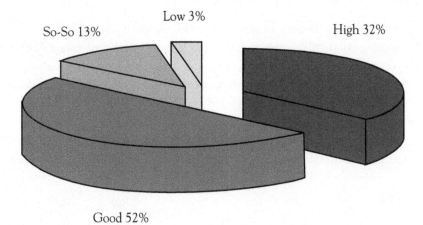

Source: Microchip Technology's Survey of U.S. Employees National averages from study conducted by the Conference Board

Figure 1.8: Job Satisfaction of Microchip's Entire Employee Population

ment. The employees concluded that Microchip practices are consistent with its stated core values (i.e., guiding values). Figure 1.8 shows that the employees had an 84% job satisfaction rate, compared to the national average of 50%. The results of Microchip's assessment are impressive and consistent with previous surveys.

Perspective

Microchip exemplifies the power of the *Aggregate System* at work. The application of the *Aggregate System* provided the foundation for the company, positioned for failure in 1990, to transform itself. Microchip's success was a result of its ability to sustain its optimum rate of continuous improvement. This superior rate of improvement allowed Microchip to lift itself from mediocrity. Microchip empowered and required all employees to continuously enhance their area of responsibility. Microchip's strategic formula and workplace values, combined with alignment and integration of everything that influences the employees' performance (e.g., culture, management, policies, and systems), united employees in achieving Microchip's mission. As demonstrated in the success of Microchip's long-term financial and stock appreciation performance, Microchip has not lost the ability to maintain its impressive rate of continuous improvement. Every aspect of the enterprise is constantly enhanced. The *Aggregate System* ensures that all desired changes are permanent and self-perpetuating.

Section Two

The Aggregate System

The *Aggregate System:*
Driving Excellence and
Continuous Improvement

IT'S CRYSTAL CLEAR to CEOs that continuously improving the enterprise is necessary to thrive in today's fiercely competitive, global marketplace. A premise of this book is that in the long run, firms that continuously improve all aspects of the enterprise position themselves for success. Where you finish is more crucial than where you started. Long-term performance relative to that of competitors depends on the company's ability to optimize its rate of improvement.

The rate of improvement applies to the entire operation, including research and development (R&D), product development, marketing, sales, manufacturing, finance, human resources, planning, legal, and facilities. A high rate of improvement yields constant advancement in products, customer service, quality, cycle times, efficiencies, cost structures, strategies, decisions, forecasting, learning curves, and so forth. These improvements ultimately drive the company's growth in revenue, profitability, market share, and stock appreciation.

Employees play a role in all improvements. Therefore, it's vital to consciously design a culture that thrives on continuously enhancing the enterprise. The culture should be built around a core set of values that articulate the firm's stance toward customers, quality, employees, profitability, and the like. The culture must motivate and empower employees to strive for excellence.

This book advocates a novel approach to the subject of company culture by viewing it as a system. As such, it can be designed, influenced, and controlled. The book describes a systematic and comprehensive approach to building an exceptional culture, called the *Aggregate System*. The *Aggregate System* is a complete system for cultivating a culture to improve the company's performance. Its purpose is to maximize the company's rate of improvement by aligning and uniting all elements of the enterprise that influence employee performance.

Competitive Pressures

The challenges involved in operating a successful business continue to escalate. Competitive pressures drive an insatiable demand to improve. In the end, the real contest lies in which firms maintain the superior rate of improvement. The further behind your competitors you are, the faster the rate of improvement you'll require. As shown in Figure 2.1, various factors are forcing companies to increase their rate of improvement: the technology revolution, increased globalization of both the marketplace and competitors, investors' demand for impressive financial performance, and the purchasing habits and expectations of consumers.

These forces have added a great deal of complexity to a company's internal systems and processes. The sophistication of these systems and processes continues to increase with the advent of new technologies and the desire for improved execution, dramatically changing the composition of the workforce. The operation increasingly requires employees to be more specialized while expanding their expertise. The complexity of the operation provides an opportunity for employees to make countless improvements. The challenge is to install a culture and systems that motivate and equip employees to continually advance the operation.

Piecemeal Approach

It can be difficult for companies looking to strengthen their competitiveness to prioritize their improvement efforts. This is especially true for struggling companies with limited capital. Should resources be allocated for

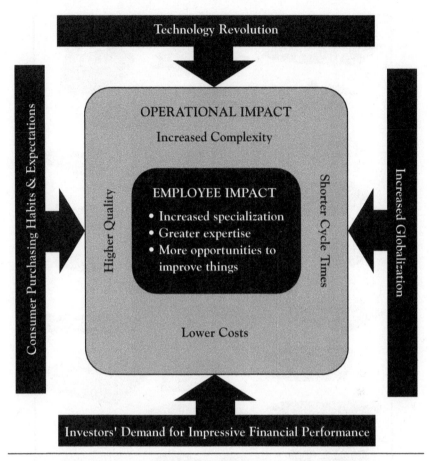

FIGURE 2.1: Some of the Forces That Drive the Necessity for an Ever-Increasing Rate of Improvement

technology investments, quality improvement programs, customer service, marketing, sales channels, planning systems, shortening cycle times, just-in-time manufacturing systems, or employee development? Companies wonder which components of the business they should enhance in order to yield the greatest return. Educators, researchers, authors, and consultants have all attempted to provide the answer, but it's still puzzling. Figure 2.2 illustrates various pieces of this puzzle.

Source: Microchip Technology

Figure 2.2: The Aggregate Business Puzzle

When the company is struggling, consultants come out of the woodwork and present their particular piece of the puzzle as the panacea. The cycle-time specialist says, "If you reduce your manufacturing cycle time, you'll lower your work-in-progress inventory, reduce capital expenditures, and uncover defective product sooner." The quality expert says, "The best return for your money is to institute my well-known quality program. This will lower costs and reduce product returns." The customer service consultant implores you to , "Get passionate about customer service." Have you noticed how the various pieces of the aggregate business puzzle go in and out of vogue?

We're confident that all these programs are well intentioned and would lend value to a business. However, if you examine Figure 2.2, it's apparent that the answer lies in the puzzle as a whole, in its aggregate, not in any single piece. Improving each piece is central to strengthening the company's competitiveness. Over the long haul, the renowned companies achieve excellence in most of the pieces.

Aggregate System

The *Aggregate System* establishes the company culture, unites employees through shared workplace values, and guides employees' strategies, decisions, actions, and job performance. The goal of the *Aggregate System* is to consciously design the enterprise to achieve its strategic formula (i.e., company's vision, mission, strategies, business plans, and P&L/balance sheet models). This is accomplished by building the company around a set of core values that will help the firm master its strategic formula. As shown in Figure 2.3, the company's policies, management practices, and human systems (how the company organizes, staffs, communicates, assesses, recognizes, compensates, develops, and advances individuals) that influence employees are aligned and integrated to these values.

The success of the *Aggregate System* in transforming the company's culture depends on the leadership abilities of the CEO and executives. They must construct the appropriate strategic formula and manage the enterprise to implement it. These leaders must role model the firm's values through their decisions and actions. They must ensure that the managers' and employees' practices are consistent with the business objectives and values. There must be no doubt what the company values, expects, and rewards.

The ultimate objective of the *Aggregate System* is to become self-perpetuating, with each element of the enterprise aligning and integrating in unison, thereby maintaining excellence. Figure 2.4 illustrates this,

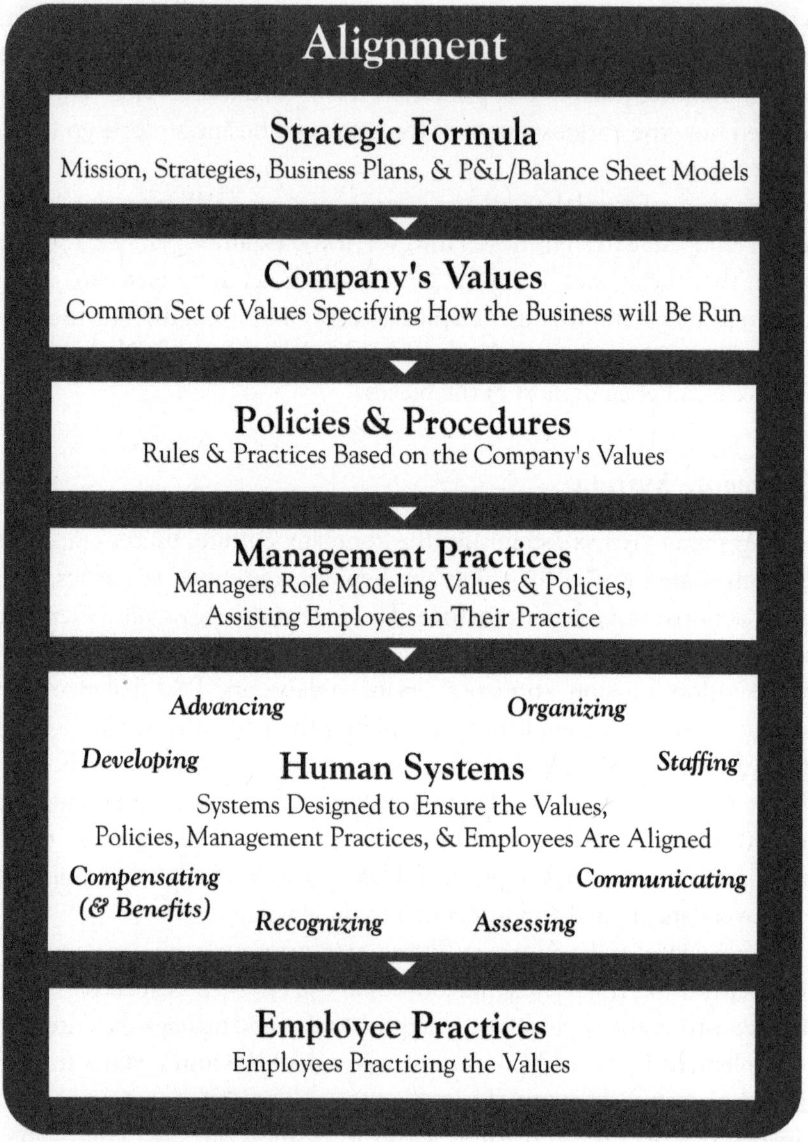

Source: Microchip Technology

FIGURE 2.3: *Aggregate System Alignment Model*

showing a conceptual model of the business processes and systems (e.g., sales and marketing, product development, manufacturing, information technology [IT], and employee development) consistently improving in a balanced fashion, propelled by the company's leadership, culture, human systems, and employees.

Strategic Formula
Vision, Mission, Strategies, Business Plans, & P&L/Balance Sheet Models

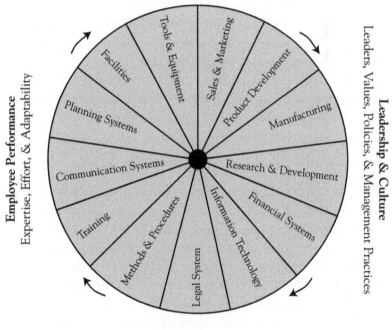

Human Systems
Systems Used to Organize, Staff, Communicate With, Assess, Recogonize, Compensate, Develop, & Advance Employees

Goal: Make the Aggregate Wheel self-perpetuating, constantly improving all aspects of the enterprise in a balanced fashion

Source: Microchip Technology
Note: Human Systems is also part of the culture.

Figure 2.4: Aggregate Wheel in Self-Perpetuation (→ symbolizes the Rate of Improvement)

The firm's adherence to its stated values must be assessed. Financial performance, quality, cycle times, customer satisfaction, and so forth should be measured utilizing traditional indicators and feedback mechanisms. However, it is also imperative to measure the employees' perceptions of the culture and the percentage of time the firm adheres to its values. This affords management valuable insights that allow for course corrections to occur.

Ideally, the *Aggregate System* works to support its blueprint for success:

Outstanding management, correct strategic formula, strong product portfolio, reputation of excellence in quality and service, terrific sales and marketing apparatus, and impressive execution of the internal operations, produced through a values-based company culture teeming with committed, empowered employees, striving to improve all aspects of the enterprise.

Employee Empowerment: Experience the Magic

The *Aggregate System* is a systematic approach designed to unleash the employees' full potential, maximizing the value they provide to the enterprise. When employees are committed and aligned to the company's objectives and values, the result can be astounding. The workforce enhances the firm independent of management's presence. Each day the workforce is engaging in countless decisions and actions to improve the company's performance. When this occurs you'll experience the magic.

The question is: "How do we attain the most from employees' expertise, abilities, and potential?" The answer is to install a culture, foster a management style, construct policies and systems, and provide training that yields extraordinary performance from the average employee. This requires empowering the employees to improve their portion of the enterprise. The employees' role must be expanded, power distributed, and communication more free flowing.

Managers need to act as coaches, developers, facilitators, and team builders. Instead of micromanaging, they need to remove barriers that obstruct employees' performance. Employees must be more involved in problem solving and strategy discussions. The employees must be given the responsibility and authority to improve their job functions. The employees closest to the actual work being performed must participate in improving that task.

Power must be appropriately distributed throughout the enterprise, rather than accumulating at the top or in the management ranks. Communication should flow throughout the organization so everyone is on the same page. Employees must be part of a continuous learning environment. Their abilities and judgment should advance as their managers coach them through each assignment. This type of approach will unleash the employees' potential.

Shared Prosperity

The compensation system must align the company's strategic formula and values, the employees' actions, and the shareholders' interests. For example, the most effective way to align the interests of employees with those of shareholders is to make the employees shareholders. Allowing employees to share in the company's prosperity is one of the primary vehicles used to build their thirst for continuous improvement. However, with the ability to benefit from the company's business up-cycles comes the obligation to participate in the down-cycles.

The compensation system normally consists of fixed components such as base salaries and health benefits. In addition, it is comprised of compensations that vary based on the firm's performance. This includes things such as stock options, restricted stock, stock purchase plans, cash bonuses, profit sharing, and retirement contributions. These varying components add essential relief to the P&L in business down-cycles.

The rewards employees receive through the compensation system must be allocated based on the merit of an individual's performance. Employees are motivated to perform because the *Aggregate System* is built on employees' relative performance and abilities within their peer group—and nothing else. Those who accomplish the most among their peer group get the most. A portion of the employees' performance assessment is based on teamwork, so they maintain a team perspective instead of becoming entirely self-interested.

Leadership

Outstanding leadership is the most critical element in the *Aggregate System*. If the leadership is ineffective or their actions and management style don't reflect the firm's core values, the *Aggregate System* will yield mediocre results. It requires tremendous talent, commitment, and sacrifice to become a strong, effective leader who consistently delivers impressive results and is respected by one's employees.

The Ten Key Elements
of the *Aggregate System*

WHEN YOU'RE CONSTRUCTING a values-based, highly empowered, continuous-improvement culture, it is essential to recognize the key elements that characterize a thriving *Aggregate System*. The key elements are an expression of the company viewed as a whole, in its aggregate form. If the company fails to achieve each of these ten elements, it won't reach its potential. Figure 3.1 lists the ten key elements that constitute the *Aggregate System*. A company's values and cultural characteristics may vary; however, each of the key elements are required to realize optimization.

1. Inspiring Leadership

The CEO and other leaders of the enterprise demonstrate the company's values through their actions—practicing what they preach. This remains true independent of economic conditions, even if it means restricting or modifying their management style or personality traits. Senior executives remain highly involved in formulating strategies and decision making, while empowering their employees to maintain and improve their portion of the operation.

The CEO tirelessly pursues the company's vision, mission, business strategies, revenue growth, P&L and balance sheet models, stock appreciation, and so forth. Moreover, the CEO holds the line on P&L margins

---

1. Inspiring leadership

2. Continuous-improvement culture

3. Clear company values

4. Fully aligned strategies

5. Employees share in the company's prosperity

6. Managers serve as role models

7. Politics, ego, and arrogance not allowed

8. Systems approach utilized to make improvements

9. Pursuit of excellence

10. Engaged board of directors

FIGURE 3.1: The Ten Key Elements of the *Aggregate System*

independent of any internal and external pressures to increase costs or lower prices. The CEO remains in touch with the market, the customers, and the needs of the community. The CEO rapidly reacts to changes in the business climate, continually positioning the company in anticipation of the future.

The CEO ensures a consistency of purpose throughout the organization—goals, objectives, and values are well understood by all. The CEO upholds lofty expectations, demanding excellence and frugality from employees. The management structure is kept relatively flat, with the lowest feasible headcount maintained. The CEO anticipates and addresses employee concerns, keeping the employees' focus on company interests rather than on the difficulties of their jobs or on creature comforts and technology tools they may desire. The CEO regularly communicates to employees on the state of the company and the marketplace.

Jim Collins' book *Good to Great* breaks leadership into five levels. The highest level of leadership is "Level 5 Leadership," in which enduring greatness is gained through a paradoxical blend of personal humility and professional will. Level 5 leaders channel their egos' needs away from themselves and into the larger goal of building an impressive company. It's not that Level 5 leaders have no ego or self-interest. Indeed, they are incredibly ambitious. However, their ambition is first and foremost for the institution, not for themselves. A Level 5 leader who is humble, listens to his people, and shares the credit is much more suitable and successful in implementing the *Aggregate System* than a self-serving, pompous leader who blames others for problems and takes all the credit.

2. Continuous-Improvement Culture

The continuous-improvement culture is built on employee empowerment and involvement, teamwork, communication, problem solving, innovation, merit, frugality, systems thinking, continuous learning, and results-oriented pursuit of success for the customers, shareholders, and employees. Management acutely understands the key characteristics of the company culture that provide the enterprise with a competitive advantage. These key characteristics reflect what the company values, what it's built around. The culture is consciously designed to foster these characteristics. The company strives to hire and maintain a workforce that is diverse yet shares similar workplace values and personality characteristics.

Since employees' workplace values, personality traits, and expertise drive their performance, emphasis is placed on values and employee development, rather than on rules. The company recognizes that excessive, or unnecessary, rules restrict continuous-improvement efforts.

3. Clear Company Values

The company clarifies how work should be accomplished by articulating its values. This provides a framework for empowered employees to operate. The company specifies its values concerning customers, quality, continuous improvement, employees, products and technology, cycle times, safety, growth and profitability, communication, suppliers and distributors, ethics, and so forth. The company is structured and shaped around these values. They serve to guide employees' strategies, decisions, and actions.

The values are convictions. They are not just appealing slogans that may or may not reflect how management actually acts. A conviction holds true even when it's not convenient and through difficult periods. The careers of managers and employees who represent the culture are accelerated. Management realizes that at times various values may conflict. Therefore it utilizes sound judgment and common sense to derive the appropriate course of action.

4. Fully Aligned Strategies

All the aspects of the company are aligned to practice its values and achieve its strategic formula (i.e., vision, mission, strategies, business plans, and P&L/balance sheet models). The company is viewed as an *Aggregate System* in which all aspects of the enterprise are aligned and continuously improved in order to master the strategic formula.

All employees are expected and empowered to improve the enterprise, and the culture is constructed to facilitate their efforts. The strategic formula specifies what is to be accomplished, while the company's values represent how the work is to be performed.

The systems, policies, and practices that affect employees' decisions and actions are aligned and integrated with the company's values to attain its strategic formula. As conceptualized in Figure 2.3, this includes aligning the company's policies, management practices, and human systems (e.g., organizing, staffing, communicating, assessing, recognizing, compensating, developing, and advancing systems) to ensure employees practice the values.

5. Employees Share in the Company's Prosperity

Employees share in the company's prosperity by aligning the interests of the employees with those of the company and shareholders. Alignment among the shareholders, company, and employees is achieved through a combination of fixed and variable employee compensation (e.g., profit sharing, cash bonuses, stock ownership, and 401(k) matching), based on individual and company performance. Alignment also occurs naturally over time as employees operate within the company's culture.

Employees appreciate the concept of total compensation, in which all sources of compensation and benefits are viewed as a whole. Through variable compensation, employees share in the prosperity of the business' up-cycles and in the sacrifices required during down-cycles. Base salary increases and career advances are given solely on an individual's merit.

6. Managers Serve as Role Models

Managers and supervisors diligently work to meet commitments, achieve the desired operational goals, and drive continuous improvement. The employees believe that the managers and supervisors consistently practice the company's culture. Moreover, management consistently promotes employees who practice the company's values. Managers, including front-line supervisors, have strong people skills, can lead and facilitate, regularly coach and remove barriers, and are comfortable with empowering employees.

Management is approachable, ethical, communicative, trustworthy, likable, adaptable, and interested in employees' inputs and welfare. Management seeks employee involvement and works to develop its employees. The employees respect their managers. They view their managers as highly competent, doing their best given the circumstances. Managers and supervisors hold employees accountable for fulfilling their job responsibilities. They have an incredible sensitivity to nurturing a "we" rather than a "we and them" (employees versus management) mentality throughout the workforce.

7. Politics, Ego, and Arrogance Not Allowed

The focus remains on the work itself, not on the personalities of the players or their desire to gain additional power. The CEO ensures that senior managers praise in public and criticize in private. Ego and arrogance are viewed as divisive to teamwork. Positive and productive team chemistry is cultivated. The traditional symbols and trappings of status and hierarchy are absent. The human resources systems and policies are designed so that these types of undesirable personality traits are not rewarded.

8. Systems Approach Utilized to Make Improvements

All aspects of the enterprise are seen as originating from an underlying system. Each system consists of input and output variables. Systems that produce undesirable results require enhancements to these variables using problem-solving techniques, statistical methods, and human expertise. Teams that consist of members with various functions or expertise are routinely formed to improve the company's systems, procedures, and policies.

As issues arise, the focus remains on fixing the underlying system, procedures, or policies rather than on immediately placing blame. Even the company's culture is consciously designed and maintained based on a systems approach.

9. Pursuit of Excellence

Employees are able and motivated in their pursuit of excellence. Employees accept and practice the company's values. They are results oriented, adaptable, and team players. They have an appetite for continuous improvement, innovation, and quality. The employees work to satisfy both internal or external customers. They thrive in an empowerment environment, which allows for greater responsibility and authority in completing assignments and making improvements.

Employees remain with the company because they like their job, supervisor, company culture, compensation scheme, and career opportunities. Employee morale and job satisfaction are valued, formally measured, and addressed proactively by management. There is a concerted effort to promote, transfer, and hire from within to advance the culture and provide career growth. Employee development is an output of the continuous learning environment. Employees work to high expectations and are accountable for their performance.

10. Engaged Board of Directors

The board of directors embraces the *Aggregate System* approach. They lead, guide, support, and motivate employees while governing the firm diligently. They are in full agreement with the company's strategic formula, culture, values, and compensation philosophy. The board works as a unified team to sustain a continuity of purpose. It maintains both a short-term and long-term perspective on the enterprise's status. The CEO and the board of directors design a compensation philosophy that aligns the interests of the employees with those of the company and its shareholders. The board members serve as role models of the company's values. They establish productive working relationships with the CEO and executives. The board members are highly qualified. Their abilities and expertise add tangible value to the enterprise. The board ensures that the company's standards, practices, and reputation remain beyond reproach by governing the firm diligently.

Section Three

The Foundations
of a Values-Based,
Highly Empowered,
Continuous-Improvement-
Oriented Culture

4

How Cultures Evolve

HISTORICALLY, CORPORATE EXECUTIVES considered the topic of company culture only cursorily. Executives have rarely utilized a comprehensive, formalized process to establish a particular culture. Rather, company cultures have typically evolved based on three primary factors: (1) the personality traits of the company's leaders and sub-leaders, (2) the rules they have imposed, and (3) what leaders have truly rewarded—which frequently has contrasted with what they've publicly pronounced. We refer to this approach as a *personality-driven culture*.

Today's executives, on the other hand, are attempting to consciously design and install a particular, desired company culture. They're not content to just let the culture evolve. However, instituting a highly successful culture entails expertise, an elaborate design process, diligence, nurturing, and periodic assessment. We refer to this approach as a *consciously designed culture*. This book illustrates how company culture is a result of a naturally occurring process, or system. Therefore, the more we comprehend this cultural system as an element of the business, the further it can be optimized.

Despite the inherent complexity and difficulties associated with instituting consciously-designed cultures, firms are embracing the approach. Executives realize that an exceptional culture provides a competitive advantage in today's worldwide, intensely competitive marketplace. For instance, all things being generally equal, companies built on continuous improvement, employee commitment, quality, customer service, and stock appreciation will surpass ones founded on entitlement and complacency.

What Is Company Culture?

Company culture refers to the governing values, policies and rules, norms, attitudes, degree of employee empowerment or decision-making authority, and prevalent management style that influence how employees behave. It's how the work gets accomplished. It's what guides employee strategies, decisions, and actions in pursuit of the company's business objectives. This is why selecting and maintaining the chosen culture is critical, with far-reaching effects.

For instance, by hiring employees who want to produce quality products, or by instilling this value within the firm's culture, you will eliminate countless problems for the company as a whole, managers and customers alike. Moreover, you'll probably obtain this favorable outcome with minimal supervision. In contrast, what is the probable outcome if you hire an employee who is not quality conscious or if your culture fails to instill a quality mind-set? Ongoing problems for all concerned.

Personality-Driven Cultures

Personality-driven cultures tend to fixate on personalities at the expense of developing a systems orientation. These cultures take on the personalities of their leaders because employees eventually decipher the leaders' personality characteristics, expectations, and what they reward. The characteristics of personality-driven cultures are as vast as the countless personality traits and the management styles of the leaders and sub-leaders they reflect.

In many instances, the leader's personality and management styles have led to terrific cultures. There are countless examples of successful personality-driven cultures. In other cases, however, this approach has caused dysfunctional cultures that impaired the company's mission and business objectives. In today's intensely competitive marketplace, not treating your culture as a system that can be optimized is shortsighted.

This section focuses on the potential shortcomings of personality-driven cultures, setting the rationale for consciously designed cultures.

Typically a business originates from one of the leader's or sub-leader's strengths. In the high-tech industry it's commonplace for companies to be founded on a novel technology or product. That's the good news as well as the bad news. Most technologists, and high achievers in general, have a personality and ability profile of "strong strengths and strong weaknesses" (see Chapter 10). Therefore, the leader can reduce the probability of the company's successes and the implementation of an outstanding culture if he fails to strengthen his weakness.

It's rare to witness a leader who has the whole package: proficiency in the technical, business, financial, customer and marketing, operational, and human elements of running a large-scale enterprise. Leaders often off-set their weakness by utilizing the strengths of another leader. Remember that high school principal who was too nice to confront the students? Instead, the vice principal was responsible for discipline. The vice principal was the one who punished students for cultural infractions.

Personality-driven cultures are inclined to yield more politics. Games of power gaining, blaming, covering one's backside, and protecting knowledge are commonly practiced. Management is apt to concentrate on criticizing people rather than quietly mounting a campaign to fix the system to prevent future occurrences. Instead of improving the system, management first thinks, "Let's find the guilty persons and berate or remove them."

Personality-driven cultures often have trouble keeping the ego power brokers and overbearing personalities in check. The company tolerates their irritating ego or belligerence because these individuals possess key knowledge or are high performers. This behavior exists because values such as sharing knowledge, distributing power, teamwork, open and honest communication, systems thinking, and excellence in people management are neither designed into the cultural system nor enforced as a rule or policy. Further, there is rarely an elaborate cultural system that holds leaders and ego power brokers accountable. The companies usually lack public statements, independent documents, and processes to ensure everyone adheres to the culture.

Eventually, employees will curtail their risk taking and will take less initiative because it's safer and easier to ask the leader or sub-leader what should be done. This directly diminishes the employee empowerment that fuels commitment to continuous improvement. Moreover, it can demotivate employees, dimming the fire within them to make a difference. It fails to develop the judgment, decision-making, and problem-solving skills of the subsequent generation of supervisors, managers, and executives.

In many cases the CEO or president may not be the true power broker. For example, you may admire a company's president but discover that the vice president heading your organization is allowed to act inconsistently. This may occur by design; it might be that the leader just tolerates this behavior. Subleaders frequently allow their own personalities to flourish with the individuals they supervise. Have you ever said to coworkers, "I wonder if the CEO knows what our boss is really like?" These types of scenarios are gradually decreasing as management styles evolve toward greater alignment with and integration into the company's values.

Consciously Designed Cultures

There are examples of success stories from both personality-driven and consciously designed companies. Nevertheless, it is beneficial to formally design and institute a culture customized for your precise business requirements and management philosophy. Your employees are too critical to the success of the enterprise not to be optimized. Moreover, why not transform them into a competitive advantage? Let your competitors struggle with employees who lack a passion for quality, improvement, and customer service. Watch them grapple with inconsistent teamwork, unremarkable performance expectations, moderate job satisfaction, and a pervasive employee-versus-management mind-set.

As every aspect of the business steadily gains complexity, consciously designed cultures are gaining popularity. Customers demand a steady stream of new, higher-value products and services, outstanding quality, excellent customer service and support, superior cycle times, and easy access to purchasing. The high demands of customers mandate that successful companies constantly improve. This growing complexity, the quest for constant systems enhancements, and the need for continuous problem solving have led to more highly educated and specialized employees. Therefore, we must design cultures that hire, develop, motivate, and retain the best employees. And the employees must share in the company's prosperity.

Numerous companies today consciously design their cultures. Intel, Hewlett-Packard, Microsoft, Procter & Gamble, Levi Strauss, Johnson & Johnson, FedEx, Southwest Airlines, Apple Computer, and IBM are but a few of these. Both authors worked at Intel for a number of years and saw the Intel culture consciously implemented. Intel's training department regularly offered classes on the company's culture. The courses helped assimilate new employees by teaching them the fundamentals of Intel's culture. Senior executives led the classes, demonstrating the importance Intel placed on its corporate culture.

Anytime you intentionally set out to systematically improve a system, the prospect of success increases. This is also true when you consciously design your culture by establishing an *Aggregate System*. A systematic approach helps ensure comprehensiveness and efficiency. As you identify the various elements and subsystems that influence the establishment of your culture, ensure that they're integrated into and aligned with the company's mission, business objectives, and values.

When we sat down in 1990 to design Microchip's culture, our goal was to consciously redesign the entire enterprise. We also wanted to truly align, integrate, and unite all company resources within an *Aggregate System* in which the company culture, systems, practices, policies, employees, strategies, decisions, and actions worked in unison to achieve our mission.

When company cultures are being designed, the trend is toward values-based cultures. As you will see in subsequent chapters, values-based, employee-empowering cultures promote continuous improvement, employee commitment, and employee job satisfaction.

Getting your key players involved early in the design of the culture promotes acceptance. It will assist you in holding people accountable for practicing the values, policies, and management style of the culture. You can say, "Hey, what are you doing? We all agreed to act this way according to the company values." It's also vital to involve employees in establishing the culture. Employee focus groups are an excellent tool you can use during the design and implementation process. This seeds the employee population with advocates of the culture.

It's crucial to periodically measure the leaders' and employees' adherence to practicing the culture. Since culture is role modeled from the leaders and is the output of an actual system, you need to formally assess the culture so that you can enhance it. Annual anonymous employee surveys are the most effective method for assessing compliance—are you practicing what you preach? If you want to avoid a "we (employees) versus them (management)" attitude, you must continue practicing a continuous improvement, values-based, highly empowered culture. A "we versus them" mind-set severely impedes the enterprise's potential performance.

The consciously designed approach is less vulnerable to leadership changes. Once the *Aggregate System* is continuously fueling the culture, it naturally grooms the next generation of leaders for succession. This phenomenon is one of the qualitative measurements that show the *Aggregate System* is in self-perpetuation. We found this continuity of succession in consciously designed cultures to be true when we worked at Intel. As the reins of leadership were passed from one CEO to another, Intel's culture was relativity unaffected. Intel's leadership has been passed on, or shared, from Robert Noyce to Gordon Moore; to Andy Grove; to Craig Barrett, the acting CEO; and now its ready to be passed on to Paul Ottelini. Even though their personalities varied greatly, they all share the core values that permeate Intel's culture. Furthermore, they were all promoted from within.

Installing an outstanding culture can be an emotionally taxing process, so remain steadfast. You'll experience progress and setbacks. Systems that drive human behavior can be complicated and are always dynamic. You seldom get from point A to point B without facing the unexpected. Reach for perfection in your employees and human systems, but don't demand it.

Rules-Based versus
Values-Based Cultures

AT THEIR CORE, human cultures, or subsets such as corporate cultures, have two basic varieties: *rules-based* and *values-based*. What distinguishes a rules-based culture from a values-based culture is the degree of emphasis placed on controlling or steering human thoughts and behavior.

Rules-based cultures emphasize establishing and documenting an extensive set of rules that govern behavior. In values-based cultures the goal is to instill a common set of values in the enterprise that guide individuals' behaviors. When an enterprise uses the consciously designed approach outlined in Chapter 4, the company's culture is constructed and managed to foster the underlying values that ultimately drive the firm's prosperity. The company values may include excellence in customer service, quality, innovation, continuous improvement, financial strength, adaptability, cycle times, technology, and teamwork.

Rules- and values-based cultures each have their virtues and shortcomings, and all cultures are comprised of a blend of aspects from both forms. The trick is to create a balance that most efficiently attains your strategic formula and reflects your management philosophy. Indeed, healthy and thriving cultures rely on an optimal blend of attributes derived from both types of cultures. The optimal form of a culture depends on both the overall circumstances and the desired outcomes of whoever is in power, be it a leader or the citizenry. For instance, exceedingly rules-based cultures tend to foster conformity, status quo, predictability, and bureaucracy. Values-based cultures tend to encourage more freedom and empowerment. This leads to greater inspiration, enthusiasm, resourcefulness, commitment, creativity, and innovation, which, when managed properly, cumulate in a high-performing and continuously improving enterprise.

Widespread improvements by the entire employee population optimize company performance. This is achieved by getting employees inspired and trained to improve their areas of responsibility. The company culture becomes a competitive advantage only when it yields exceptional performance out of the average employee. It must also allow the high performers to thrive as well as effectively deal with low performers.

Excessively Rules-Based Cultures

Rules are necessary to bring structure and order to societies, companies, organizations, and families. The enterprise, and the individual, desires some sense of structure, uniformity, constancy, and predictability provided by rules. For instance, we expect other drivers to stop at a red light, and we want highly detailed policies and procedures for employees who are operating nuclear power plants. We need rules to set boundaries for our children. Soldiers might not "take that hill" if they were not indoctrinated into a strict rules-based culture that doesn't allow them to opt out of the mission.

Policies, procedures, specifications, regulations, and mandates represent company rules. An executive's or supervisor's management style is often a personification of the organization's rules and norms. For companies, the extent of formal rules depends on how critical the operation is, the organization's responsibilities, the level of an individual's position, and an individual's job duties. In normal circumstances employees operate just fine within the rules of the firm. A particular group of employees may not like a given rule, but in general everyone adapts to the rules.

However, the company's rate of improvement is impeded when employees perceive the rules as excessive. By their very nature, excessive or unwarranted rules and a representative management style tell employees not to change things. Employees reason, "If management defines and controls everything, it doesn't like change." The excessive rules-based culture creates psychological barriers, a reason to "not fully commit to the organization's improvement goals." When management doesn't seek, ignores, or fails to act on employees' suggestions and attempts to improve the operation, the employees become discouraged. At every turn employees need to overcome a non-value-added policy or procedure. They conclude that it requires too much energy to make a change.

Excessive Rules Grow Bureaucracies

As is true for many large corporations, government institutions are often overly rules-based. Recall your last visit to the Department of Motor Vehicles or the Social Security Office. Did you observe others' dissatisfaction with the degree of bureaucracy, or experience it yourself? The insidious by-product of bureaucracies is that employees grow insensitive to the customer (in this case, us). Moreover, even on trivial matters these employees lose their desire and ability to think outside the box.

Last spring Michael went to the Department of Motor Vehicles to resolve a minor matter. Blue and red lines were painted on the floor to guide people to the various counters. From the signs it was not obvious if he should stand in a blue or a red line. He looked for a help desk, but none was to be found. So Michael stood in the blue line. As he patiently waited in line for forty minutes, he wondered why the employees were behind wire mesh walls. And he thought, "What's with that large sign that states no cursing or shouting at clerks?"

Finally, Michael reached the counter. He was greeted by a woman whose body language told everyone she had long ago lost interest in helping others. She proceeded to inform Michael that he was in the wrong line. She said, "You should be in the red line." He replied, "I'm sorry, but this appeared to be the right line based on your perplexing signage. It's only a simple matter. Could you assist me?" She replied, with a tone of voice suggesting she'd given this reply to countless others, "No, I said you needed to be in the red line." She then shouted, "Next." He hurriedly asked, "Since I've waited forty minutes in this line, could I go to the front of the red line?" She replied, "No. Policy requires you to go to the back of the red line." Now he realized why she was behind the wire mesh and discovered the inspiration behind the no cursing or shouting sign.

Rules-Based Management Style

On occasion the organization becomes too rules-based due to a supervisor's management style. To consciously or subconsciously satisfy a personality trait, the supervisor may unwarrantedly micromanage employees. This trait can stem from a need for excessive control, an inability to trust others, or a need to be perceived as the smartest. A rules-based management style can lead to unnecessary or exhaustive policies, procedures, and specifications, creating an environment where it's difficult to truly empower employees. The rules-based mind-set assumes that additional rules fix problems.

The Big Picture

We can easily see the contrast between excessively rules-based cultures and values-based ones when we look at various forms of government. Historically, Communist governments and dictatorships have reflected excessively rules-based cultures. Their rules or laws may extend to where you will live and work, your occupation, acceptable discourse, access to healthcare, and availability of governmental resources. The ramifications of not following these rules can be harsh or even deadly. People then lose their inspiration to take ownership to improve the status quo and instead concentrate on adhering to the rules.

These forms of government have demonstrated their inability to build a continuously improving society. The former Soviet Union personifies the depth to which years of indoctrination and fear can affect people. Russia is struggling in its attempt to achieve greater freedom and capitalism. People's beliefs and values are slowly shifting in response to their new environmental conditions. This shift from a rules-based to a values-based mind-set will be the fuel that leads to improvement in all aspects of the country.

The United States government reflects a healthy and effective balance between values and rules. America was founded with a values-based emphasis. This can be seen in the Constitution and the Bill of Rights. Over time the U.S. government has continued to add rules (e.g., policy, laws, and regulations) when the Legislative and Executive branches of the government deemed necessary. It is natural for values-based cultures to become more rules-based over time.

Consciously Designed Values-Based Cultures

In values-based company cultures, the enterprise is designed around what it truly values: customers, quality, profitability, technology, distributors, partnerships, employees, continuous improvement, innovation, cycle times, communication, teamwork, employee empowerment, and so on. These values are clearly stated, defined in detail, and communicated to employees. This is exemplified in Microchip's stated value on quality:

> **Quality Comes First:** We will perform correctly the first time and maintain ISO 9001 and QS 9000 quality system certification to ensure customer satisfaction. We practice effective and standardized improvement methods, such as statistical process control, to anticipate problems and implement root cause solutions. We believe that when quality comes first, reduced costs follow.

Values serve as a beacon in the night. They are where discussions begin and to where wayward discussions return. The company values guide employees' strategies, decisions, and actions.

The Tylenol incident several years ago illustrates this point. After finding that some of its product had been intentionally contaminated, Johnson & Johnson pulled Tylenol from store shelves nationwide. This was a drastic action, as many businesses would have pulled only product from the geographic area specifically affected. However, in deciding it was better to be safe than sorry, Johnson & Johnson conveyed that two of its core values were consumers' health and confidence in its brand. The company acted in accordance with its values independent of the enormous short-term financial impact to the firm.

Aggregate System

In consciously designed, values-based cultures the values are instilled using some variation of the *Aggregate System* approach. Just stating your values is not enough. The company's policies, systems, procedures, and training curricula must be constructed to realize these values. In a controlled environment such as an organization, most people will adjust to the circumstances and act accordingly.

At Microchip, a core value is "Continuous Improvement Is Essential." This value is woven deep in the fabric of its *Aggregate System*. The realization of this value can be seen in the company's prosperity. It also can be seen in the day-to-day interaction with employees. For example, employees attend a course that teaches Microchip's culture. The CEO initially taught the course. It is now taught by the directors and vice presidents, occasionally by the CEO, and offered every quarter. Executives teach the course to demonstrate how important the culture is. Moreover, it reinforces to directors and vice presidents that they too should "walk the talk."

The class attendees are operational directors, managers, engineers, secretaries, factory personnel, and so on. They represent a true cross-section of the firm. When teaching the course, we would always ask the employees to tell the class one improvement initiative their organization was tackling and one thing they were personally working to improve. Seldom did an employee fail to provide a fine answer. Everyone was involved in some form of continuous-improvement activity. This was one of the numerous minor indicators that the *Aggregate System* was in self-perpetuation. The desired culture was real.

Uncovering a Company's Values

Corporations express their values in many ways. If you're astute these values will quickly become apparent. To illustrate, Steve recently made changes to his investment portfolio, which necessitated interaction with two large well-known banks located on the West Coast. A certificate of deposit (CD) had matured at both banks and he wanted to close out his accounts. He experienced two separate sets of corporate values. The values were manifested in the employees' demeanor, policies, and the robustness of their systems to serve the customer.

The first bank made it as inconvenient as possible to close out Steve's CD. He had to personally go to a branch and wait in line for 20 minutes. The person he worked with clearly did not care if he closed the account or renewed it. One thing he did not like about this bank was that it no longer provided customers with certificates stating the renewal terms. He had rarely heard of such a ridiculous practice at any financial institution. The bank told him that it no longer provided these statements because it was an administrative burden but, not to worry, he was in the system. The entire experience reinforced why he didn't want to do business with that firm. Its values, policies, and systems were designed to make everything more convenient for the bank, not the customer.

The second bank was a pleasure to do business with. It provided Steve with appropriate statements, took care of the transaction on the phone, and encouraged him to renew his CD or place it in another of its investment products. The individual who helped Steve was interested in serving his needs, and the bank's policies were convenient. The institution's values, policies, and systems were designed to make everything more convenient for the customer, not the bank. So he went ahead and renewed his CD for another year. Steve witnessed two different firms' performance on the same stated values: convenience and customer service.

Values Are Always Present

The leaders' values are always present and impact the work environment. Employees soon come to understand the company's values whether or not they are publicly articulated. The leaders act according to their personal and professional values and beliefs. Intentionally or not, the leaders role model, and the system rewards, what the enterprise values. Therefore, it's more efficient to articulate the firm's values and build the organization around them than to just let the company evolve. This is one reason why it's so effective to consciously design the culture.

Stated versus Practiced Values

Some companies' stated values are inconsistent with what they practice. Michael used to work at a firm that continually stated that quality was its top priority. However, it soon became apparent that its true value was: "We always tell everybody that quality is paramount; however, we ship everything to make the numbers even if the quality of the parts is questionable. Never, and I mean never, miss the forecast." In this case, the company would have been better off to never state its values in the first place. Employees resent hypocrisy, leading to a diminished impression of management.

If the firm can't state its true values it may be that they would not be well received. Hence, many politically charged firms as well as companies that are not focused on the customer, employee, shareholder, or quality know it would be foolish to state their true values. Could you imagine a business publicly stating that its goal was to gouge the customer whenever possible, that employees are a necessary evil, or that excellence in quality costs too much?

If you're disappointed with a company's service, how do you ascertain if it's the fault of the company culture, internal systems, or the particular individual you're interacting with? Repeated contact at several points in the enterprise will provide the answer. Cultural and internal systems issues represent systemic problems, visible throughout the organization.

Here's a story that illustrates a case where the values given to the employees were too rules-based and not values-based enough. A few years ago, Steve bought his daughter a personal computer from a large international corporation. He also purchased a three-year warranty on the machine. After a couple of years, the Ethernet board was not working, so he called the warranty service for repairs. The help desk happened to be in Bombay, India, and it was difficult to get technical support. After a lot of hassle, the company agreed to send a technician to Steve's home and replace the Ethernet board. However, even after the technician did so, Internet access still did not work.

The technician deduced that the Web browser software program was corrupted and needed to be reinstalled. The technician told Steve that he was not authorized to work on reinstalling the Web browser program. He knew how to reinstall the program but needed authorization. His job was to change the Ethernet board, which he did. Steve asked him to call technical support. The call was made and they reached Bombay once again. It was the middle of the night in Bombay and the support person had no authority to authorize the technician to reinstall. The technician yelled at the technical support person that he was not being helpful. At that time, the technical support person hung up the phone. The technician left Steve's home without fully fixing the problem. The technician could easily have fixed the problem and left Steve satisfied, but the company's excessive rules did not allow for this. The result was that Steve never bought a computer from this company again.

Values Drive Behavior

As we will see in Chapter 9, behaviors stem from values. Thus, influencing someone's values will lead to countless actions that support those values. Consequently, if you can get the employees to practice the company's values when conducting company business, the entire population will be working in unison to realize the strategic formula. Shared values are the glue that holds cultures together. Corporate cultures are no exception.

The vast majority of us don't send our children to school just because it's a rule (law). We send them because we value education and to improve our children's futures. If we didn't have locks on our doors, would the majority of us break into our neighbor's house? No, we wouldn't, because it's illegal. Our values tell us it's wrong. The store clerk who is courteous and helpful to the customers, independent of the company's watchful eye, is doing so because he values excellence in serving others. This is the type of employee you want to hire. In this case, both the company and the employee value customer service.

Company Values and Personal Values

It's important to understand you're not trying to change people's personal values. You're requiring management and employees to adopt the company's values when doing the company's business. You're communicating the company's doctrine to the employees and, therefore, what the company rewards. You're not directly asking employees to alter their personal values. Outside of work they can express their values as they choose.

The key is to hire individuals with similar workplace values as the firm's. Such people will readily adapt to the culture and will require less supervision and training than those whose workplace values differ from the company's. This will make life easier for all parties. Occasionally, however, the company may hire an individual whose skills are critical to the operation but whose personal values are not in sync with the stated corporate values. In such cases, it requires significant training, monitoring, and coaching to ensure that such an individual's performance remains high while not negatively impacting the culture. Often, such people's workplace values will not completely change. Therefore, managers must ensure that their actions and decisions stay within an acceptable deviation. Make sure that their strong weaknesses do not overcome the strong strengths for which they were hired (see Chapter 10). People are individuals, after all, not machines. No two individuals are the same. Some deviation from the norm is acceptable. Beyond that, individuals must be held accountable.

Multinational firms must tailor the *Aggregate System* and their corporate culture to specific countries. It may be unrealistic to attempt to have a foreign group practice the corporate culture in every aspect. Maintain the firm's core values worldwide and allow local management to customize additional workplace values and systems based on each specific country. For example, in the early days of building Microchip's culture and systems, we came across numerous differences between the United States and Western Europe. The labor laws, vacation days, national holidays, retirement contributions, use of stock options, and personal taxes all varied from country to country. We could not design one system in the United States and expect it to be accepted and effective in every European country.

Transitioning from Rules-Based to Values-Based

The transition from an overly rules-based culture to a values-based culture is difficult but achievable. Managers and employees will be skeptical that management and the culture will change. Some employees will embrace the change, others will watch from the sidelines, and a few will resist. The leaders must convey their sincerity and commitment to the new culture. The *Aggregate System* must be systematically and conspicuously employed to demonstrate the change is real and to ensure its permanence.

Excessive rules can create psychological boundaries that lead employees to give up on attempts to make improvements. This phenomenon is sometimes referred to as *learned helplessness*. Learned helplessness represents the conditioning of humans or other species to maintain the status quo even when it's not in their or others' best interest. They have learned to give up on things such as striving to make swift and continuous improvements.

A simplistic illustration of learned helplessness is the classic mouse and electric charge plates experiment. A mouse is placed in a box divided into two sections or chambers by a short Plexiglas wall. Electric-chargeable metal plates line the bottom of the box. The experiment begins by sending an electric shock to the plate beneath the mouse. The mouse's natural reaction is to leap to the other side of the box. Momentarily the mouse experiences relief. However, the mouse then receives an electric shock from the plate beneath its feet. So the mouse jumps back to the other side of the box. This is repeated until the mouse learns that relief comes from jumping to the other side of the box.

Now the experimental conditions are modified by delivering an electric shock to the plates simultaneously in both chambers of the box. Initially the mouse attempts to gain relief by jumping to the other chamber, but no relief comes. The mouse frantically jumps back and forth, but receives a shock by whatever course of action it takes. Eventually it gives up and stops jumping to the other chamber for relief. The mouse just stands there and takes it.

Once again the conditions change. The electric charge is turned off to the chamber in which the mouse is not standing. How do you think the mouse responds to this new condition? It continues to stay stationary even though relief is just a jump away. The mouse has learned to be helpless to improve the situation by making a change. This is the same thing most of us would do.

When a company is transitioning to a values-based culture, the CEO personally needs to lead the employees out of this phenomenon of learned helplessness. The leader of the enterprise must inspire the troops to become empowered continuous improvers. While the leader role models the new culture, he or she should regularly communicate with employees on the status of the changes. Thus, as the frontline managers practice the core values, and as the company's systems are aligned within the *Aggregate System*, learned helplessness will gradually disappear.

Prior to 1990, Microchip maintained a rules-based culture. We had to personally oversee the company's transition to a values-based culture. When we started doing so, there was a lot of fence-sitting by many employees, including several executives. Most employees tended to see the coming visionary changes as another fad that would pass if ignored. We therefore learned that a successful transition requires relentless and inspiring leadership that drives the culture and role models the values. Initially, progress may come slowly and backslide easily with the smallest of missteps. However, the end result will be worth the effort.

6

Systems Thinking

AT ITS CORE, *systems thinking* is a perspective, a way of viewing the world. You seek to comprehend all of the factors that contribute to a given phenomenon or outcome. This allows you to view the outcome in its aggregate. Systems thinking is based on an understanding that most things can be explained in terms of a result that stems from or is influenced by one or more underlying systems, each of which is composed of inputting factors. Therefore, if you want to change a given result, you must: (1) understand the factors that constitute the underlying systems, (2) employ an effective method for changing them, and (3) successfully modify enough of the underlying systems to achieve and sustain the desired outcome. It requires effort and discipline to comprehensively analyze phenomena in their aggregate.

You need to ask and answer questions such as "what's causing this condition, or *norm-state* (current set of conditions), to persist?" and "what aspects of the aggregate must permanently change so that the desired result is produced?" Only with the establishment of a new and self-perpetuating norm-state will change take hold. Failure to sufficiently align enough of the underlying sub-systems with the desired outcome is the primary reason why corporate initiatives, the desired culture change, and the collective employee performance goals are not realized.

Systems thinking is prevalent in the fields of engineering, astronomy, physics, and biology. It's less widespread in the fields of psychology and management. Many of us view human behavior, personality traits, values, attitudes, motivations, and abilities as difficult subjects to truly comprehend. The source of such human attributes is often not directly observable. And when it comes to group or societal norms and cultures, the landscape is even less discernable.

However, if we set aside a person's free will and the inherent random events that impact our lives, we can use a systems orientation to explain and modify many of the individual and cultural attitudes attributed to humans. From this basis came the origins of the *Aggregate System*, in which the company's culture is seen as a system. As such, the culture can be consciously designed to optimize the probability of achieving its strategic formula (i.e., mission, strategies, business plans, and P&L/balance sheet models). Thus, the culture can provide a competitive advantage if all the elements that influence employees are aligned and integrated to empower employees in the pursuit of excellence.

Effective employee empowerment requires structure in such things as company values and policies, performance management, systems thinking, and problem solving methodologies. It's essential that empowered employees be provided with both the culture and tools conducive to sustaining continuous improvement.

Why Corporate Initiatives Fail

Why do so many corporate initiatives fail or seem to fade away? Why do we say, "The more things change, the more they stay the same?" We've all experienced the new corporate initiative, served up with copious fanfare and glitter and introduced with inspiring speeches coupled with banners encouraging the troops to improve quality, utilize statistical process control, reduce costs, shorten cycle times, improve customer service, "work smarter, not harder," and/or sell an unpopular product line.

The vast majority of senior executives' expertise lies in creating and achieving the company's strategic formula. Boards of directors don't hire a CEO unless they're convinced the prospective candidate will be able to fulfill the company's strategic formula. However, CEOs and executives frequently find it difficult to fully execute the initiatives or targeted changes.

Resistance might stem from managers, employees, systems, policies, existing company culture, or logistics. Therefore, once you are assured of the initiative's correctness, the question becomes, "How do you effectively create and sustain the desired change?" The answer is held within the *Aggregate System*. Let's rephrase the question to ask (1) "What's the most effective approach to convey the need for, and merit of, the desired changes?" and (2) "How must the company's systems, policies, and management practices be designed to ensure that the changes last?" This book answers these two questions by describing a total system for establishing a culture that is orchestrated to embrace change, to get managers to role model the change, and to have systems that reinforce the change.

The norm-state is always supported by a host of contributing factors. Hence, a sufficient number of the factors that contribute to the norm-state must be modified to maintain lasting change. Sustaining a change and establishing a new self-perpetuating norm-state can be an arduous task. If the change is contrary to the norm-state, the other contributing factors will assert enough force to bring the situation back around to its original state. Thus, the more things change, the more they remain the same. Even at the most superficial level, it should be obvious that initiatives that are not rewarded by the current systems, policies, and management practices won't take hold.

Attack the System, Not the Person

The fundamental approach of systems thinkers is to attack problems and initiate improvements by analyzing the systems or conditions that produce the undesirable outcome. The first reaction is not to punish the person who made the mistake, but rather to improve the system so it does not happen again. If a worker knocks over material onto the factory floor, the initial questions should be, "Has this occurred previously?" and "How can the work stations be laid out to avoid a recurrence?" In this type of environment, employees are more likely to bring problems forward. Furthermore, it minimizes managers consuming valuable time trying to protect themselves because of an employee mistake.

Using Brute Force

Brute force is occasionally needed to achieve an objective. If managers are not systems thinkers and a critical activity falls behind schedule, they'll often achieve the desired result through brute force. They'll apply so much attention and emotion toward the employees that the project will be pushed to completion. Frequently the employees overcome the system in achieving the objective.

The limitation of this approach is that you overcome, instead of improve, the system. Based on human nature and the other factors that maintain the previous norm-state, the gains will be short-term. This is not of concern if the activity is a one-time event. However, seldom does brute force translate into improved performance over the long haul. If no one fixes the underlying weaknesses in the current system, the next person may well recreate the undesirable outcome.

When brute force turns into a management style, it results in poor working relationships with employees and inconsistent performance. Further, when the employees leave, the system will require the unpleasant process of brute force to begin all over.

Human Tendency: Focus on One Dominant Factor

Many people don't like to think in systems terms, or to take a systems view, because it requires difficult thought and effort. Moreover, some people get overwhelmed when attempting to analyze the numerous factors that contribute to a given outcome; it often adds additional complexity that they can't, or don't want to, deal with. Further, it frequently makes the solution appear more complex and perhaps even unsolvable.

Most people prefer to remain concentrated on what they think is the dominant factor causing the undesirable outcome. For example, if a school district is performing poorly, the parents may say it's the teachers' fault. The teachers may conclude it's the parents' fault, while the administrators say it's the politicians' fault for providing insufficient funding. The politicians announce it's the media's fault, and so forth. The answer is that, in general, all these parties are probably contributing to the failing system. Therefore, each sub-system (e.g., parents, teachers, administrators, politicians, and media) needs to analyze and modify the factors that affect their sub-system. Then the larger educational system, in its aggregate, can realize sustained improvement.

The problem with our tendency to fixate on one or two factors to explain or improve an undesirable outcome, especially those relative to humans, is that the norm-state is maintained by several contributing factors. You seldom sustain change and establish a new self-perpetuating norm-state by modifying only one of the contributing factors. Usually the other factors will assert enough force to bring the situation back around to its original norm-state.

The Evolution of Systems Thinking

Historically, employees had little involvement in defining the systems and procedures that govern their work. This has slowly changed over the years as operational complexity has increased. Increased complexity has caused employees to become more specialized and to gain greater expertise. Moreover, it has vastly expanded the opportunities for employees to make improvements to the operation.

As shown in Figure 6.1, this gradual transformation toward tapping the inputs of employees began with employers asking employees to solve a particular problem. The issues were typically contained and specific in nature. The underlying systems and sub-systems that comprise the enterprise were addressed by experts. Today, it's commonplace for employees to be knee-deep in systems improvement activity. We expect employees to provide input concerning how things can be enhanced.

Perfectly Designed

"Every organization or system is perfectly designed to get the results it's getting." Why is this statement profound? This is one of the most perceptive statements we've come across in our many years of studying and practicing management. The statement is at the heart of the nature of continuous improvement cultures, which preach, "If we don't like the results we're getting, let's take responsibility for understanding the issue and improving the contributing factors." It leads managers to three conclusions:

1. Even if we can't see it, an underlying system that is contributing to the result is always present.
2. Therefore, we must assume responsibility for the current result and improve the underlying system.
3. These improvement efforts necessitate a systematic methodology rooted in problem solving techniques, statistical methods, and human expertise.

We recall a meeting at Microchip in which we discussed low employee morale at one of our manufacturing plants. The management team was struggling with the issue. Each team member was working long hours and felt they'd done a great deal towards meeting the employees' needs. So naturally the management team began to feel unappreciated, concluding the employees held unrealistic expectations. Michael chimed in, saying, "Well, we've developed a perfect system for generating low morale." We then asked, "Okay, what actions can we take to improve our understanding of the situation and what methods should be employed to increase

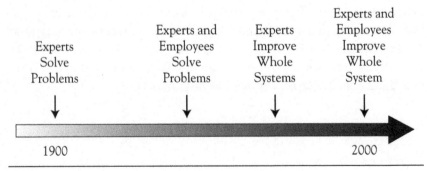

FIGURE 6.1: Evolution of Systems Thinking

morale?" We analyzed the factors that contribute to employee morale so we could conceptualize them as a system. The necessary modifications were implemented and the desirable outcome was realized.

A System Is Always Present

Even though we're constantly immersed in systems, their presence isn't always evident. Michael stumbled into this realization while earning his Master's degree. In the afternoons, he'd congregate with friends in front of the library. They'd linger outside the library to postpone hitting the books. Their favorite bench overlooked the main thoroughfare. The bench's weathered wooden planks concealed its true value. It afforded them a grand vista for people watching.

During one of these study sessions, Michael noticed that students venturing from the library to the adjacent science building had worn a dirt path right through the manicured landscape. In their rush to class, students had trampled a flowerbed, two hedges, and the lawn in front of the entrance. This was a shame. The students were scarring the beautiful grounds.

This scarring hadn't gone unnoticed by the groundskeeper. A feud between the groundskeeper and the hurried students was brewing. By the spring semester the battle between the nonconformist students and the perturbed groundskeeper was in full swing. The groundskeeper's initial tactic was to post a sign in front of the flowerbed. It read, "Please stay on paved walking paths." This met with no success.

The groundskeeper then upped the ante by stringing a yellow rope in front of the flowerbed, looped through green sticks. A new sign that said, "Keep Out" hung tautly from the rope—there was no politeness this time around. It took only two days before the rope and sign were lying on the ground, soiled by the footprints of numerous students. Throughout the semester the quiet skirmish of erecting, and re-erecting, trampled signs and barriers continued.

Witnessing this dispute upon his perch on the weathered bench prompted Michael to wonder, "What's really happening here? How could this whole escapade have been avoided?" He concluded the original architects gave insufficient consideration to two factors: attitudes and values of the student population, and the presence of the system for walking the campus.

Regarding attitudes and values of students, in general, college students aren't big on following rules. They've entered their rebellious, independent stage. They're not going to be inconvenienced, or late to class, because of a rope or a sign. They could easily have walked on the paved path to the entrance. It wasn't that much further. But they placed greater value on convenience than on a nonscarred landscape.

As for the system underlying campus navigation, if the architects had given greater consideration to the existence of this navigation system, the scrimmage between the groundskeeper and students may have been avoided. In designing a foot transportation system, the architects had several alternatives. They could have enlisted students to provide input on the most effective layout of the walking paths. They could have taken the most direct path between each building to place the paved paths. They might have even allowed students to walk to class a few times, paving the trails they forged. In this way, no student would ever deviate from the prescribed path.

The point of this story is that an underlying system is always present. This one consisted of walking paths and students' walking preferences. If the architects had initially comprehended all the factors that contribute to these systems, the landscape would have remained pristine.

Taking Responsibility for the System's Results

The knowledge that underlying systems are always present, and they produce the current condition, shifts our mind-set from victim, and thus helpless, to assuming responsibility for improving the system. Responsibility starts with converting the issue into a problem-statement using the word "perfect." For example, "We have a perfect system for angering the customer, and for producing poor-quality products, excessively long R&D development cycles, low margins, unreliable computer networks, low productivity, high turnover," and so forth.

You know you're on the right path when a team member says, "The systems couldn't produce any other result because the inputting factors or variables that constitute the underlying systems were consciously or unconsciously designed to produce this result. We're getting what we've designed the system to get. It couldn't be any other way. Now how do we modify the underlying systems to produce the results we desire? We've developed a perfect system for long cycle times; now let's develop a perfect system for short cycle times." It takes guts to make these types of statements in a meeting. Nevertheless, when employees make such statements, it often becomes obvious that rather than being a victim of the situation, the team is responsible for changing the systems to produce a more desirable outcome.

Improving Systems Requires Methodology

Improvement starts with utilizing a structured methodology. Figure 6.2 describes a systematic problem-solving process that structures the employees' improvement efforts. All employees should receive training on the problem-solving methodology the company employs. This facilitates its usage, establishes a common language, and reinforces the desired culture. Depending on an employee's job responsibilities, additional training on specific problem-solving tools may be compulsory. Problem-solving tools range from such things as using statistics, statistical process control, measures of central tendency, frequency distributions, percentages, probabilities, design of experiments, and so on.

Additionally, standardized approaches and methodologies are especially critical in a highly empowered, improvement-oriented culture. It's vital that the employees understand the importance of data and consensus in decision-making. Just because employees are empowered doesn't mean they can go around making changes based on their opinion alone.

Input and Output Variables

The primary intent in discussing input and output variables is not to present a refresher to your college science 101 course. The purpose is to ilustrate how these basic concepts are directly applicable to designing cor-

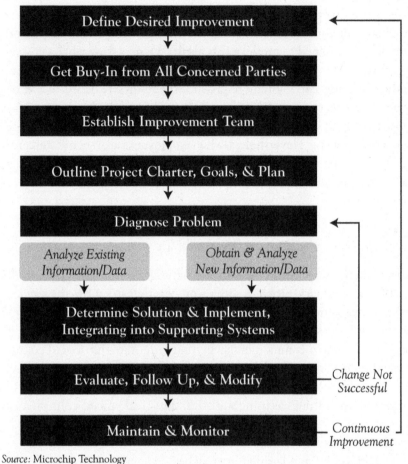

Source: Microchip Technology

Figure 6.2: Problem Solving Process

porate cultures and optimizing employees' performance. It's an avenue to provide further structure to the "gray areas" associated with human behavior and culture.

A fundamental concept that must be part of any problem solving training is *input* and *output variables*. Input variables are the factors that contribute to the outcome or output. So, input variables represent those things, or factors, that produce or influence the situation. The output variables are those things being influenced—the final result or effect. For example, let's say that the output variables associated with an outstanding cake are its appearance, taste, and texture. The input variables are such things as the amount of sugar, flour, and butter. Other inputs to making a divine cake are the heat of the oven, the baking time, and the competence of the decorator.

The term variable is frequently used to describe a factor or outcome. This is done because it exemplifies the inherent variability, and the quest to measure this variability, associated with contributing factors and resulting outcomes. Output variables can be changed only if you change one or more of the input variables. For example, you can't make the cake taste sweeter by telling it to sweeten up. The cake will gain additional sweetness only if you add more sugar or reduce the amount of the other ingredients (input variables). We'd like to be able to just tell the output variables to improve. However, it takes effort and discipline to identify, measure, and modify the input variables.

Life is a chain of input and output variables. Most output variables are an input variable to something else. The output variables associated with an outstanding cake may be input variables for someone's weight problem or pleasure in life.

Another example of input variables can be seen in the steps involved in manufacturing computer chips. When computer chips are fabricated, thin films are deposited on the surface of the wafer (substrate). This can be achieved by heating gases in a vacuum tube or chamber. As shown in Figure 6.3, the input variables are such things as the length of time the device stays in the chamber, the temperature of the chamber, the type and quantity of gases, the rate of flow of the gas, and the pressure within the chamber. These input variables all have a direct impact on the output variables of the film's thickness and uniformity.

When examining the system of corporate culture, you need to comprehend and orchestrate the input variables so that you attain the desired outcomes. Let's say that the output variable of teamwork is desired. First you must identify the input variables that influence the practice of teamwork. Figure 6.4 shows some of the input variables associated with instilling and maintaining teamwork. This includes such things as hiring team players, management role modeling, rewarding teamwork, training team

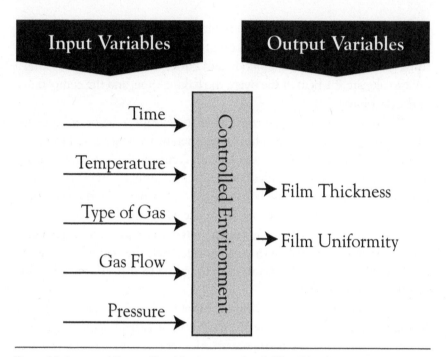

Figure 6.3: Input and Output Variables Associated with Thin Film Deposition

skills, tying cash bonuses to achievement of team goals, offering stock options, building sufficient conference rooms, and providing tools for employees to communicate. Next you must align and integrate the input variables within the company's *Aggregate System* (e.g., values, policies, human resources systems, management practices). In this way the practice of teamwork will be realized.

The Underlying Systems and Variables Associated with Educational Achievement

What are the underlying systems, including the input and output variables, associated with a child's educational success? And what can children teach us about designing corporate cultures? Let's imagine that after reading this book, you've decided that your family unit represents your *Aggregate Sys-*

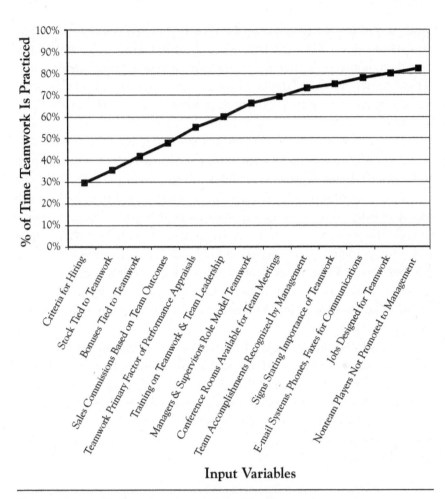

FIGURE 6.4: Input Variables Associated with Instilling Teamwork

tem. This inspires you to purchase flipcharts and gather the family around the dining room table. You inform the group that you've decided to consciously design the family. As you finish your proclamation, the wife rolls her eyes, the children scurry in all directions, and the dog interrupts his slumber, lifting his ear inquisitively.

Once the group reassembles, you begin by constructing a mission statement: "Maintain a loving family that works for the betterment of the group while respecting the uniqueness of each member." The family then agrees to a set of values: "Caring relationships, health, financial security, education, communication, friendships, integrity, accountability," and so forth. These values are then translated into value statements, including your value statement regarding education: "Education is essential to a successful life."

The conversation turns to defining the input and output variables associated with the value statement. First, the output variable is established: a Bachelor's degree from an accredited college. Then you ask, "What are the input variables that'll increase the probability that the children will graduate from college?" The responses come flying in. "Pay us for good grades," the youngest boy shouts. "Give me a car and I'll go to college next year after graduating from Jefferson High," declares the eldest daughter. Mother says, "What about defined study times, limiting television, reviewing homework, saving money for college, and visiting the teachers more?" The final list of input variables your family constructed is shown in Figure 6.5.

Successfully completing the list of input variables shown in Figure 6.5 won't guarantee that the output variable, obtaining a Bachelor's degree, will be reached. Realization of the educational goals could derail due to a child's personality traits and interests, financial hardships, learning or physical limitations, or some other random event. Meeting the requirements of the input variables list, however, significantly increases the likelihood of success.

Start Them Young

The field of astronomy is a marvelous avenue to introduce children to systems thinking. When Michael's children were young, he'd have them recite their home address using the universe as the end system. He'd ask them, "Where do we live?" They'd respond, "Come on, Dad, not again." Then they would say, "Okay, we live in the universe, in the Milky Way galaxy, in the solar system, on Earth, in North America, in the United States, in Arizona, in Phoenix, at 1125 Ash Avenue." Michael's purpose

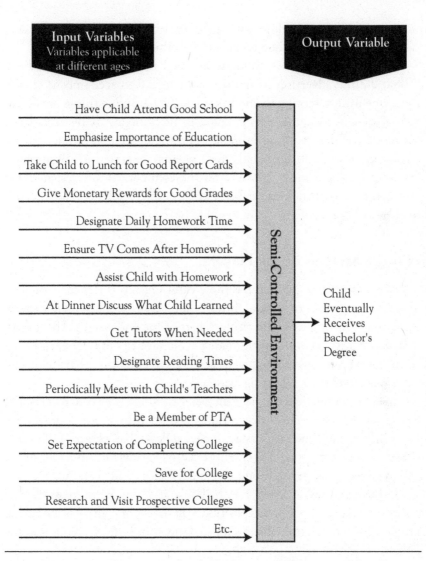

FIGURE 6.5: Input Variable Associated with Child Eventually Obtaining College Degree

was to provide his children with a perspective of the systems and sub-systems that constitute their address within the universe.

When Steve and his children watched television, he'd ask them, "What did the advertiser design this commercial to accomplish? How is this company attempting to condition you? What subtle things are occur-ring to influence you to use its product? Is the company trying to associate the product with something desirable or prestigious, tap into your basic in-stincts, or make you think you'll have a pleasant experience?" By attempt-ing to gain insight into why and how the commercial was designed, the children exercised their critical-thinking, problem-solving, and systems-orientation skills.

Is It the Systems or the Players?

A classic question is "Which has the greater impact: the systems the em-ployees work within or their abilities?" Our answer is that we view every-thing that contributes to the result as part of the end system. This means that in order to maximize performance, you have to optimize each of the contributing sub-systems (e.g., values, management, systems, policies, and employees) and their inputting factors.

Let's take a simple example. Phil Jackson, at one time coach of the Los Angeles Lakers and the Chicago Bulls, is one of the premier coaches in NBA history. He's known for coaching great basketball players, for his spe-cific coaching style, and for his highly effective triangle offense. One of the main features in his triangle offense system is to pass the ball into the cen-ter. If the center has an open shot, he'll take it; if not, he will pass the ball back out to one of the shooters positioned at the perimeter. This system has produced several championships for Jackson with both the Bulls and the Lakers.

But you say, "Wait a minute. He had some of the best players in NBA history. That's why they won." It is true he had some of the best players in NBA history. So, was it the players, Phil Jackson's coaching style, the tri-angle offense system, or even the ownership and the front office that pro-duced so many championships? Our answer is that they're *all* sub-systems of the *Aggregate System* for winning championships.

Bad systems do indeed hinder high performers. And even the best systems often can't compensate for dreadful performers. We think that outstanding managers or coaches make the greatest impact when the employees or players are average performers. What all the great coaches and systems have in common is their ability to generate extraordinary results from an average set of players. This is especially true in corporations, where consistently outstanding results are often achieved by placing average employees in an excellent system. This topic will be further explored using the employee performance output equation described in Chapter 19.

A Word to the Wise

Be careful that a company decision to change from one system to another is not being done because it promotes an employee's career aspirations or because people have just grown tired of the inherent negatives of the current system. Steve's been asked, "Which is a better approach, this one or that one?" If the two approaches are both reasonable, he replies, "The answer doesn't intrinsically lie in the merits of the system, but rather in the quality of management it'll receive." In life you get what you manage. Great managers can make either of these two reasonable systems successful. The question should be restated as, "Can the manager effectively manage in a fashion that decreases the inherent shortfalls associated with the system selected?" If so, select that system.

In the case where you choose a system or approach among a group of potential options, all relatively equivalent in their advantages and disadvantages, the human tendency is to initially be excited by its newness and advantages, and downplay its disadvantages. However, over time, the inherent negatives begin to wear on the group and the previous system may regain its appeal. The point here is that when selecting among alternatives, remember that the best one may be the one that's best managed. Keep in mind that change doesn't necessarily equal improvement. Therefore, work to ensure that all your changes result in sustained improvements, not just more change.

The Six Principles of Building a Merit-Based, Variable, Total Compensation System

EMPLOYEES REPRESENT BOTH a valuable resource and a considerable expense to a company. Each of the components that contribute to the employee's total compensation system must reinforce attaining the company's strategic formula, practicing its values, and satisfying the shareholders' realistic expectations. Specifically, the components shown in Figure 7.1, along with the rest of the elements of the *Aggregate System,* motivate and retain employees. A merit-based, variable, total compensation system best achieves the company's strategic formula while maximizing the employees' potential overall compensation.

While base salaries may remain fixed, other components of the employees' total compensation must vary based on business conditions. These varying components add essential relief to the P&L in business downcycles. More importantly, they allow employees to participate directly in the company's prosperity by giving employees a stake in the company's success—a piece of the action. The total compensation system reaches optimization when it gains self-perpetuation—the strategic formula is realized due to the employees' dedication. In turn, when the company prospers, so do the employees and shareholders, furthering their commitment.

Employees must be compensated and succeed based on their abilities and contributions. Continuous-improvement cultures, rooted in employee

- Base salary
- Salary merit increases
- Employee cash bonuses
- Management or key personnel cash bonuses
- Profit sharing plans
- Stock options or restricted stock
- Stock purchase plans
- 401(k) or retirement company matching
- Sales incentives
- Paid holidays
- Paid personal and sick time

- Vacation days
- Overtime pay
- Shift differential pay
- Medical and dental benefits
- Short-term and long-term disability benefits
- Life and accidental death insurance benefits
- Mental health benefits
- Health club membership reimbursement
- Onsite and offsite training
- Tuition reimbursement
- Paid sabbaticals
- Alternative health care

FIGURE 7.1: Sample of the Various Components that Constitute a Total Compensation System

empowerment, flourish in environments founded on merit only. Employees quickly lose enthusiasm and commitment if they see that compensation stems from such things as length of service or favoritism, rather than the merit of their performance. The various components that constitute an employee's total compensation should derive from a mix of individual performance, team performance, and company performance.

This chapter is not intended to introduce novel total compensation components, but rather to ensure that these components facilitate the alignment and self-perpetuation of the *Aggregate System*. This is achieved by designing a merit-based, variable, total compensation system according to the six principles shown in Figure 7.2.

The Total Compensation Approach Requires Belief

The underpinnings of a merit-based, variable, total compensation system are the employees' belief in the success of the enterprise, and the rewards they will receive as a result of that success. When employees lose their belief in the pending, or continued, success of a company, the benefits associated with the total compensation system are lost. In fact, employees may jump ship for a higher base salary or a better total compensation system offered by a more attractive firm. Start-ups, newer, or smaller companies must work to maintain the employees' belief in the firm. Well-established companies with outstanding track records typically don't have to deal with doubts or credibility issues.

We've been asked, "How long does it take for the components of the total compensation system to allow the *Aggregate System* to reach self-perpetuation?" This depends on too many factors to provide a simple answer. It could be one year or four years. The most critical factor during

1. A merit-based, variable, total compensation system is the system most conducive for achieving the company's strategic formula, by maximizing the employees' potential overall compensation.
2. The total compensation system consists of fixed components that remain stable and variable components that vary according to the company's performance.
3. The total compensation system incorporates a blend of an individual's, the team's, and the entire company's performance.
4. Pay practices and scales are competitive and based on the criticality and rarity of the expertise.
5. The company provides employee health care, insurance, and retirement benefits, with employees sharing in the costs and responsibilities.
6. Education and communication are essential for employees to understand and appreciate the total compensation system.

FIGURE 7.2: The Six Principles of Building a Merit-Based, Variable, Total Compensation System

this gap between the company's current performance and the anticipated success lies with the leadership abilities of the CEO. The CEO must build and maintain the employees' confidence in the company's continued or pending success. Moreover, the CEO needs to clearly articulate how the employees will benefit from the company's prosperity.

While we were at Intel, we saw how President and CEO Andrew Grove's leadership maintained the employees' confidence in the company's continued success. There were years such as 1985, when the semiconductor market and Intel's performance nose-dived in the wake of a serious shake-up in the personal computer marketplace. It required Andy Grove's personal leadership to maintain employee confidence.

We saw a similar scenario at Microchip. During the early 1990s, when Microchip was transitioning from being a money-losing operation to achieving significant success, not all the employees could visualize success on the horizon. Substantial sacrifices to resize the company needed to be made. It required significant leadership from Steve, and considerable organizational development support and advice from Michael to maintain employees' confidence. The moment of success came with the highly successful initial public offering (IPO) of the company in March 1993.

In short, strong leadership is the short-term glue required to maintain and inspire the team. In the long term, the *Aggregate System* will take over and satisfy this objective. However, remember that companies go through economic and business cycles. Employees tend to buy into variable compensation easily during an up business cycle and usually want higher fixed compensation during down business cycles. Therefore, the leadership of the CEO and executives, as well as the support of Human Resources, is needed to continuously sell the variable compensation program.

It's Rarely Just about Compensation

Other parts of the *Aggregate System* beyond total compensation must also work in concert to motivate and retain employees. For example, employees need to feel they're continuously learning and developing, that opportunities for career advancement are present, they like the company's culture, and they like their supervisor. The main reason employees initiate a job change is they dislike their supervisor. The *Aggregate System* is built on numerous elements that yield maximum results, and self-perpetuation relies on these elements operating in unison.

The Six Principles

The six principles that a merit-based, variable, total compensation system is founded on are discussed below.

1. A Merit-Based, Variable, Total Compensation System Is the Most Conducive for Achieving the Company's Strategic Formula through Maximizing the Employees' Potential Overall Compensation.

The total compensation system must produce alignment among the company's strategic formula and values, the employees' actions, and the shareholders' interests. This allows all parties to benefit through revenue growth, profitability, and stock appreciation. For instance, the most effective way to align the interests of employees with those of the shareholders is to make the employees shareholders. Employees should share in the company's prosperity through such things as stock options, restricted stock, stock purchase plans, cash bonuses, profit sharing, and retirement contributions. These types of compensation directly motivate and retain the employees. When the company is doing well, the employees are doing well. When the company experiences long-term success, both the employees and the company yield greater prosperity from an approach that combines fixed and variable compensation components.

The *Aggregate System* is advanced when the company shares its prosperity with the employees. With the sharing of the prosperity comes sharing of the commitment to excellence. Giving everyone a stake in how well the company performs also creates a culture of "we" rather than one of "we versus them" (i.e., employees versus management). Therefore, the objective is to spread the components of the total compensation system as widely and deeply as possible throughout the enterprise. Executives will find that when the employees have a stake in the business, the executives' personal prosperity increases.

In the *Aggregate System*, a substantial portion of the employees' overall compensation can be derived from components other than the base salary. Therefore, compensation must be viewed from the perspective of one's total compensation, rather than just the base salary. The expense to the company and financial gains attained by the employee through the components shown in Figure 7.1 must be considered when employees determine their true compensation. The overall goal should be to beat your competitors in the employees' total compensation, not in base salaries alone.

The total compensation system must be *merit-based*. This means employees are awarded such things as salary increases, stock options, and promotional opportunities based on their abilities and performance. Employees are motivated to perform because the *Aggregate System* is built on employees' relative performance and abilities within their peer group, and nothing else. Those who accomplish the most among their peer group get the most. Well-known methods such as ranking and rating, which rank employees' performance, and assigning ratings (e.g., outstanding, successful, or needs improvement) relative to their peer group, can be employed to determine the merit of employees' contributions.

2. The Total Compensation System Consists of Fixed Components That Remain Stable, and Variable Components That Vary According to the Company's Performance.

The total compensation system must consist of a mixture of components that remain fixed and stable and components that fluctuate in their real or potential value according to team and company performance. *Fixed compensation* consists of components such as base salaries, medical benefits, any guaranteed retirement plan matching by the company, and tuition reimbursement. Holiday, vacation, and sick pay are also forms of fixed compensation. *Variable compensation* consists of components such as stock options, restricted stock, stock purchase plans, employee cash bonuses, management cash bonuses, variable profit sharing or retirement plan matching contingent on the company's performance, sales incentive plans, and so forth.

The company's objective is to make variable as many of the compensation components as is practical. This will facilitate employee commitment and decrease the harshness of any unpleasant actions necessitated by down-cycles. Everyone, from the factory worker to vice president, shares in the prosperity of the up-cycles and sacrifices in the down-cycles. This is accomplished by having a meaningful portion of the employees' total compensation in the variable category. An additional advantage of variable compensation is that during the down-cycles, employees understand why these components provide little income. Consequently, employees' emotional reaction to lower total compensation is vastly reduced, helping maintain morale.

When employees accept a job with substantial variable compensation, they're not fixated on securing the highest base salary. They are opting to join an exciting or prosperous company that is providing acceptable fixed compensation with the potential upside gains offered through the variable components. The variable compensation approach works only if the employees eventually realize actual gains or continue to believe in the future success of the enterprise.

At the time of an acquisition, if the acquired employees' fixed compensation is too high, transition some of the employees' fixed compensation into variable. If this is not practical, give a portion of their future salary increases in the form of variable compensation. For example, they will receive a reduced annual merit salary increase, but will now be eligible for the employee cash bonus or management bonuses that are variable. If you automatically add all the variable compensation components to newly acquired employees with high fixed compensation, you're adding additional compensation without the employees participating in any downside jeopardy.

International companies must remember that each country will have different compensation components based on what is competitive and customary. Therefore, avoid adding all the United States plans to the international workforce until you have conducted a comprehensive analysis.

3. The Total Compensation System Incorporates a Blend of an Individual's, Team's, and Entire Company's Performance.

The various components that constitute employee total compensation should derive from a mix of individual performance, a team performance, and company performance. The more you design the system toward a team-oriented model, the better. This greatly facilitates teamwork and helps everyone moderate the natural tendency to think of themselves too much and the team too little.

Individual-based compensation components or awards are such things as base salary, salary merit increases, and sales commissions. Psychologically, it is important to ensure that an employee's salary merit increase is designed as an individual component. People perceive base salary and salary merit increases in very personal terms. Moreover, individual-based compensation provides employees with a sense of financial stability and allows them to structure their lifestyle. Attempting to turn salary merit increases into a team-based award is not pragmatic.

In 1996, we at Microchip sensed that the sales process in the semiconductor industry was going global. In many cases, customers designed our product into their systems in the United States, but then they would subcontract to Asia for manufacturing. Therefore, after a U.S. salesperson had worked hard to get the account, it would be handed over to a salesperson in Asia who would receive commissions on the subsequent large manufacturing orders. In this environment, Microchip's U.S. sales force became increasingly frustrated. The salespeople felt they weren't getting paid commissions for their work because the customer moved the account offshore. Moreover, in many cases, we would see Microchip's Asian sales force quote lower prices to woo the customer to buy in Asia. This caused Microchip to compete with itself to capture the sales commission.

To deal with this problem, many companies in the semiconductor industry have implemented split sales commissions. This is where the credit for a given commission is shared between the original location (where the account was initially won) and the manufacturing location (typically in Asia). In 1996, Microchip was the first company, and it remains the only one we know of in the industry, to eliminate sales commissions entirely. Veteran sales executives in the industry disagreed with us, but we took a systems approach to the problem. We put our salespeople on the same bonus plan as our management team. Their job then became to win the global sales game together. The Asian sales force no longer quoted lower prices to win business away from the U.S. sales force to earn higher commissions, because their bonus was based on the company's overall performance (i.e., results of the entire workforce/team). Microchip devised a slogan, "One World, One Team, One Goal. Make Microchip #1." Since then, Microchip has been one of the most successful and profitable companies in its line of products, becoming number one in 8-bit microcontroller unit shipments in 2002, as shown earlier in Figure 1.6.

Team- or *company-based* compensation components are such things as stock options, restricted stock, stock purchase plans, and cash bonuses based on quarterly performance of the company or a specific business unit. Other team- or company-based components include the variable portion of the company's matching of the employee's 401(k) contributions, profit sharing plans, and the company's formula for the management bonuses.

When the culture of empowerment, teamwork, and continuous improvement is strong enough, individualized sales incentives beyond merit increases may not be needed. Under some circumstances, individualized sales incentives for sales personnel can decrease the overall effectiveness of the sales system. As demonstrated in the Microchip example previously, sales commissions or bonus plans based on the company's overall results can yield better results.

4. Pay Practices and Scales Are Competitive and Based on the Criticality and Rarity of the Expertise.

The company's pay practices and pay scales must be competitive with those of the companies that attract your employees, along with the criticality and rarity of the field of expertise. If you have a thriving total compensation system, it makes no sense to pay base salaries on the high side of the competitive range. In contrast, unless you're an exciting startup, you won't be able to attract desired candidates if your base salaries are not competitive. The key is to find the appropriate balance between fixed and variable compensation for your specific circumstances.

5. The Company Provides Employee Health Care, Insurance, and Retirement Benefits, with Employees Sharing Costs and Responsibility.

The company should provide affordable employee health care, insurance, and retirement benefits comparable to those of its competitors. With the soaring costs of health care, employers must require employees to share the expense. It will continue to be taxing for both the employer and employee to absorb the dramatic annual inflationary increases demanded from health-care providers, as a solution to the rising costs of health care is nowhere in sight.

The primary objectives concerning employee healthcare benefits are: (1) select quality providers with competitive cost structures, (2) design the plans to allow employees to choose various levels of coverage with corresponding premiums, (3) have employees share in the costs, (4) communicate the company's expense specific to each employee by incorporating these costs into the employee's year-end total compensation statement, and (5) attempt to encourage employees to adopt healthy lifestyles.

Avoid adding too many costly features to your plans. This will only compound the issues associated with the inflationary nature of the healthcare industry. Employees have difficulty accepting large rate increases for their medical and insurance coverage. Further, since employees tend to perceive benefits as an entitlement, removing features can produce a negative backlash.

The days of employers fully funding their employees' retirements are ending. Companies are requiring employees to take greater responsibility for their retirement planning. This means accumulating savings they will need during retirement and managing their retirement portfolio. The use of 401(k) plans has become pervasive. These plans allow employees to save pretax dollars up to an annual maximum (i.e., $14,000 for 2005), and the monies grow tax-free until distribution. Most employers will match some portion of the employee's contribution to encourage participation in the plan.

6. Education and Communication Are Essential for Employees to Understand and Appreciate the Total Compensation System.

You must continually work to keep the employees appreciative of their total compensation. This is accomplished through education, communication, and information. Employees need to receive training that explains stock options or restricted stock, the stock purchase plan, cash bonus plans, and so forth. In particular, employees need to be shown periodically the actual value and potential value of the variable compensation components.

A merit-based, variable, total compensation system with all its various components is foreign to many employees. Odd as it may seem, even in the high-tech world, many employees do not fully understand how such things as stock options work and how to place a value on them. When you provide stock options to your average factory worker, the issue is even more pronounced.

A portion of the employee population will fail to appreciate the total compensation approach. For example, some executives might say, "I am underpaid because my base salary is too low," even though their total compensation is several times their base salary and probably the highest in the city for their specific position. Or an engineer might say, "Stock options are an employee benefit, not part of my total salary." Companies can combat this mind-set by periodically showing employees the value and potential value of their total compensation.

It's vital to provide employees with annual year-end total compensation statements. These statements detail the actual value and potential value of each of the compensation components. Figure 7.3 illustrates an abbreviated version of Microchip's year-end statement. The employees are often surprised to see the value of their total compensation as a percent of base salary.

Employees need help judging the future value of their variable compensation components. Along with giving your employees their year-end

*This Total Compensation Statement is a summary of the **"potential value"** of the Company's compensation and benefit programs. This personalized statement reflects your benefit elections as of 12/31/04*

Employee: John Doe

Salary Components:	Value to Employee
Annual Base Salary:	$$
Miscellaneous Salary:	
Shift Differential:	$$
Overtime:	$$
Misc. Allowance:	$$
Total Value of Salary Components:	**$$**

Cash Bonus Components:	
Bonus Pay:	
Employee Cash Bonuses:	$$
Management Cash Bonuses:	$$
Total Value of Cash Bonus Components:	**$$**

Stock Components:	
Potential Stock Purchase Plan Gains:	$$
Potential Stock Options Gains:	$$
Total Value of Stock Components:	**$$**

Benefit and Retirement Components	
401(k) Plan:	
Employer Matching:	$$
Pre-tax Savings on Deferral:	$$
Tuition Reimbursement:	$$
Health Club Reimbursement:	$$
Paid Time Off:	
Vacation:	$$
Personal & Sick Absence:	$$
Holidays:	$$

FIGURE 7.3: Example of Year-end Annual Total Compensation Statement

Benefit and Retirement Components

Health Care and Benefit Plans:	Company's Contributions	Employee's Contributions
Dental Plan:	$$	$$
Vision Plan:	$$	$$
Short-term Disability:	$$	$$
Basic Employee Life:	$$	$$
Accidental Death and Dismemberment:	$$	$$
Long-term Disability:	$$	$$
Alternative Health Care:	$$	$$
Total value of Benefit and Retirement Components	$$	

Your Total Compensation (Salary, Bonus, Stock, and Benefit Components): $$

Your Bonus, Stock, and Benefit Components Represent This % Above Your Base Salary): $$

Additional Benefits Not Cited

In-house training, subsidized cafeteria, group universal life insurance, group legal plan, travel accident insurance, credit union membership, U.S. Savings Bonds payroll savings plan, direct deposit, relocation expenses, non-taxable tuition reimbursement, and warehouse club memberships.

The estimated value of the stock programs is based on the FMV $$ of the company's stock as of 12/31/04. The stock calculations are based on the assumption all vested stock in 2004 was held until 12/31/04. The value of the stock programs will fluctuate with the market value of the stock.

Source: Abbreviated version of Microchip Technology's Total Compenation Statement

FIGURE 7.3: Example of Year-end Annual Total Compensation Statement (*continued*)

statements, provide them with a stock option forecast statement. Determine a realistic annual stock appreciation rate—let's say 15%. Then construct a statement that shows the number of stock options vesting each year for the next five years and their annual value based on a 15% annual growth rate. Also, show the employees what the cumulative value of the stock options would be if they chose not to sell them until the fifth year.

The company should provide a history of its stock performance as a reminder to employees. At the same time, it should provide a disclaimer that stock prices fluctuate and that the estimates presented are not a guarantee of future performance.

Stock Options

Stock options are not stock. Stock or equity is what you purchase from one of the stock exchanges (e.g., the New York Stock Exchange and NASDAQ). *Stock options* are a granting of a specific number of shares that, once vested, provide the employee the option to purchase the shares at a set price. The set price is usually the closing price of the stock on the day the stock options were granted. The stock will vest (become available to the employee to purchase) according to a specified vesting schedule; for example, four years.

If the hard work of the employees has resulted in a higher stock price than when the stock options were granted, the employee can purchase them from the company at the original set price and sell or hold the stock—the gain is the employee's. If the stock price has not appreciated or if it has gone down from the set price, the employee will realize no financial gain—the risk did not pay off.

From a historical perspective, this is a great time for the average worker. In the past, the average worker rarely received a piece of the action. Only the executives of the company were eligible to participate in stock options or ownership programs. Employees' commitment to the enterprise's success and prosperity has come with sacrifice and hard work. The money the average employee has received from stock options has paid for their children's education, homes, cars, contributions to charities, and so forth.

Stock options fueled the emergence and continued growth of the high-tech revolution. Over time investors have benefited handsomely from the fruits of the high-tech laborer. This revolution has given humankind countless benefits.

This sweat equity that employees gain through increasing the value of the stock price has pushed them to develop technologies that have improved all of our lives. Profits from stock options have funded countless new start-up companies. Moreover, they have given these start-ups a vehicle to compensate and motivate their employees.

Characteristically, start-ups are cash poor and hire employees who accept lower fixed compensation for a chance to get a piece of the action if the company is eventually successful (unfortunately, most are not). Many of the companies that achieve success continue to provide employees with stock options to motivate and retain key personnel. The *Aggregate System* strives to provide all employees with a stake in the company's prosperity through stock options.

The Federal Accounting Standards Board (FASB) has ruled that with the fiscal year starting after June 15, 2005, stock options will have to be expensed on the company's income statements, according to the Generally Accepted Accounting Principles (GAAP). Companies should now be careful not to throw away stock options. If stock options have been a part of the *Aggregate System* for years, they should be evaluated with the new rules on expensing. Any changes should be carefully designed not to disrupt the *Aggregate System*, including the concept of variable compensation. Many companies may adopt restricted stock plans rather than stock options plans. Unfortunately, it may result in fewer employees receiving options. The lower-level employees may cease to participate altogether.

Stock Option Systems

An effective stock option system requires a systematic methodology for allocating and granting stock options. It must be well thought out and competitive. The system utilizes matrixes that specify the number of options new employees are to receive. This number is based on an employee's job category (e.g., engineer, administrative, sales) and grade level. For example, all senior engineers (grade 12) will receive 1,000 stock options at hire contingent on board approval. They will vest over four years, vesting 25% annually (i.e., 250 shares per year).

Many companies make the mistake of giving employees options only at the time of hire. When employees' options are fully vested, they are no longer locked in. Even if they ask for, and receive, additional stock options, it may take years for the new shares to significantly appreciate in value. Since stock prices tend to appreciate over time, the further out in time the option vests, the greater its value at the time of exercise/purchase. Therefore, be careful to ensure that vesting occurs over a long period of time (four to five years).

Evergreen stock systems are designed to provide existing employees with additional stock options each year. The number of shares employees receive is based on matrixes similar to the one described above for new hires. However, an Evergreen matrix only specifies an annual run rate for each position (e.g., senior engineers should vest 100 shares per year). These shares will vest 5 years out. Employees receive additional stock options each year to maintain their annual run rate. Ultimately, this system locks in the employees. The system ensures employees are never without 5 years of stock vesting in front of them, as illustrated in Figure 7.4. This is an excellent example of one of the systems that makes the *Aggregate System* self-perpetuating.

General Observations

During the down-cycles, utilize stock options to maintain employee good will. If you can't afford annual salary merit increases, convert the proposed increase into options that vest the following year. In addition, options are a great vehicle to say "thank you" to employees for their hard work. Company-wide "thank you" stock option grants have an extraordinarily positive effect on employees and reinforce a teamwork, results-oriented culture.

CEOs are frequently hesitant to grant employees additional stock options during down-cycles. This is when the stock price is depressed. This

Stock Option Vesting Schedule
(For one employee over time)

Grant #	Total # of Shares Granted	Year Shares Granted	2006	2007	2008	2009	2010	2011
New Hire	400	2005	100	100	100	100		
First evergreen	100	2006					100	
Second Evergreen	100	2007						100

- Assumes the employee was hired on January 1, 2005
- Company uses an annual vesting schedule (shares for each year vest at the end of that year)
- Individual's yearly run rate: 100 stock options
- Shares in this illustration refer to the number of stock options granted

FIGURE 7.4: Example of Stock Option Vesting Schedule Using an Evergreen Employee Stock Option System

tactic hurts the *Aggregate System*. In the long term, the employees always benefit from low option prices and it will increase your locked in factor during the next up-cycle, the period when competitors will court your employees.

Design your employee stock purchase plan to have two-year offering periods and the ability to purchase shares at a discount. Be sure to limit the participation rate of employees to ten percent of their base salary or you will burn through too many shares. A two-year plan means that the stock purchase price will remain constant for two years for the employees who entered the plan at the initial entry period. Most firms use six-month offering periods and the right to purchase the stock at a discount. This two-year fixed purchase price plays a tremendous role in employee motivation, job satisfaction, and retention.

It's important to have your employees view stock options and bonuses as part of their compensation, rather than as part of the benefits plan. If this is not achieved, employees may consistently feel they're underpaid. You will hear, "The company pay is just okay, but it has great benefits." Avoid this by following the advice provided in principle six: Education and

Communication Are Essential for Employees to Understand and Appreciate the Total Compensation System.

Reasonably moderate, more frequent rewards to the employees are better than infrequent, larger ones. As with any good relationship, keep the employees satisfied and they will have no need to look elsewhere. Therefore, design as many of the compensation components as possible to pay out quarterly. Moreover, timely rewards are more effective than annual rewards. For example, even though Figure 7.4 illustrates an example where the employee received stock options vesting annually, we think it's more effective to have them vest monthly. Do the same with your employee and management cash bonuses, and any variable contributions to employees' retirement plans. When the company's quarterly performance is good, so are the accompanying rewards for employees.

The Issues Surrounding Stock Options and Recruiting

When recruiting, you'll find that candidates can be influenced by the total number of stock options they're offered from the various companies at which they're interviewing, without understanding the likely value. Candidates have said, "I want 50,000 stock options because this little start-up down the road is offering me that much." They make this demand even though the start-up company will probably never go public. If it does, the stock price may never substantially appreciate.

Candidates are often unduly influenced by the brand name of the company rather than evaluating the company's stock price performance. The bottom line is that candidates have difficulty placing a realistic value on the potential value of stock options. The recruiters in Human Resources need to be able to enlighten them.

Finally, from sports, there is a saying, "Winning cures everything, while losing magnifies every little issue." When the *Aggregate System* is correctly operating, stock price appreciation cures countless issues. Just like winning does in sports.

How Managers Become Barriers

Eleven Management Styles that Impede Employee
Empowerment and Continuous Improvement

THIS CHAPTER DESCRIBES the various management styles that obstruct the establishment of a values-based, highly empowered, continuous-improvement culture. Each of these management styles negatively affects employee empowerment, negatively affecting continuous improvement. Moreover, these impeding styles discourage employee involvement, commitment, enthusiasm, job satisfaction, development, decision making, and appropriate risk taking. Managers become barriers when their management styles are not conducive to the desired company culture.

If any of the management styles described in this chapter reflect your style, utilize the Human Change Process, outlined in Chapter 11, to structure your development. To varying degrees, most managers incorporate a portion of each of these styles within their management style. The trouble arises when any specific style becomes so pervasive that it produces undesirable results. Additionally, certain circumstances may warrant managers to temporarily adopt one of these styles. Therefore, be careful to avoid unduly categorizing your unique management style with one of the styles discussed in this chapter. Remember that the most effective management style is one that's tailored to the specific employee and circumstance. Different circumstances require different management styles.

The "I Need to Review Everything and Participate in All Decisions" Manager

This management style represents the classic micromanager, who creates an inefficient bureaucracy by becoming the bottleneck to the organization's improvement objectives. This is the over-controlling manager who meticulously tracks projects, is in the loop on all decisions, and has to put his or her stamp on everything. Since practically every proposal, strategy, and decision must go through this manager's office, the manager becomes a barrier to the group's productivity and rate of improvement.

Advice

If this typifies your management style, you'll benefit from resisting the temptation to be involved in everything. First, set a goal to systematically reduce what you're currently reviewing. Determine the critical points or conditions under which you still need to intervene. Then inform your employees of the new approach. For example, tell them, "When projects get more than two weeks behind schedule, please call a meeting so I can better understand the situation. If there are no issues, just update me in our monthly one-on-one meeting."

Ensure that you clearly outline your expectations of the employees concerning their newly gained empowerment. Then step back and see the benefits of increased employee empowerment. Continue allowing greater empowerment, coupled with just the right amount of coaching. Instead of having employees do something because you asked them, make projects their responsibility and help them (but remember, not too much). This will increase each employee's level of commitment to the success of the project.

Tell the employees why you're adopting this new style. Ask for their help by having them let you know when they feel you're micromanaging. It's only natural that employees may fear providing you with this type of feedback. Therefore, pay attention to your verbal and non-verbal communication when receiving the feedback. When the employees finally get the guts to tell you you're micromanaging again, let them know that you've heard, and appreciate, their feedback.

Overcoming this style of management requires that you resist your need to be in control. Remember that if you want to be an outstanding manager, it's not about you and your needs; it's about the employees and their needs.

The "Answer" Manager

This represents the manager who's always ready to provide the answer to everyone's issue. Such managers think that since they're in charge, it's their job to give everyone the solution to the issue at hand. Moreover, since they used to do that job, they know what's best. This manager could be called the "I'm right" or the "My way is the best way" manager. This style of management is frequently associated with individuals who aren't good listeners. The main problem with this style is that it stops employee involvement, creativity, and growth. Employees never feel empowered because the answer is always provided. Moreover, few of us learn by being told something. We require the experience of trial and error for something to truly sink in.

Advice

If being the answer manager is characteristic of your management style, and you'd like to bring your style more in balance, we recommend that you first control the temptation to provide the answer. Then, practice being more of a coach. Convince yourself that what you should take pride in is not your own contributions, but those of your employees (this will allow you to keep focused on their development and provide a rationalization for not getting your immediate needs met).

It's often easier and more enjoyable to give the answer as you see it to employees, rather than coaching them as they discover the solution. Inherently, there's nothing wrong with providing solutions for your employees. However, it's important to find a balance between the criticality of the situation and the need to grow and motivate the employees. Make sure you're not providing the solution just because you like doing it, or because it's easier.

If you want to build and maintain a strong, competent, committed, and enthusiastic team, you'll have to put the gratification of fulfilling some of your needs on the back burner. For example, you may feel good when you come up with the answer to someone's problem. It may give you a sense of importance, prestige, job security, or just challenge. It may even be the thing you like most about your job. However, a manager's true job is to build and maintain a team that achieves excellence. So keep the focus on making every employee a stronger and more robust performer.

You must learn to facilitate the employees in their discovery to uncover the answer. The best technique for accomplishing this is to keep asking questions that lead them to the solution. These questions should be geared at helping the employee uncover the factors contributing to the issue and the potential ramifications of a decision or action. Become masterful at asking leading questions that allow employees to see the situation more clearly. You can do this by utilizing a series of non-threatening, inquisitive questions. "Have you thought about this?" "How are you going to deal with this or that item?" "Who do you think you need to talk to?" Then use leading questions to fill in the gaps where the employee has fallen short. "Do you think that maybe you should talk to John about this?"

You'll know this approach is working when employees frequently come to you on their own to discuss what they're thinking or planning. They're doing this because it adds value, not because you have the answer. This is the time you can also practice your influencing and coaching skills. Help employees learn to play "one chess move ahead" when formulating strategies and decisions. From time to time, you'll have to tell the employee what to do if the wrong solution leads to unacceptable ramifications.

The "I'm Only Measured on Operational Output" Manager

This is the management style of someone whose focus is always on the operation and seldom on the employees. Such managers think that as long as the operational indicators (such as output, quality, and cycle times) are strong, everything's okay. Their focus is to excel in those areas in which they're measured. Since most companies don't measure human indicators beyond absenteeism and turnover, such managers often don't concern themselves with employee empowerment, involvement, development, or job satisfaction.

In addition, over time this type of manager frequently comes to view employees as a pain, not an asset. Such managers are so busy focusing on the results of the operation, they have little tolerance left to deal with the human aspects of it. Typically, it takes a major crisis originating from the employee population before they're willing to modify their management style.

Advice

If this is your management style, our first recommendation is for you to step back and reflect on the true value of the employees' contributions. Second, in business we measure what's important to us. We have measures to indicate customer orders, sales revenue, manufacturing cycle time, product quality, and so forth. You should establish indicators for measuring employees' concerns, perceptions, and job satisfaction. This data will motivate management to address valid issues and provide feedback on the effectiveness of the culture and management practices.

Frequently, this type of management style derives from an individual who is not a people person. Such managers either don't like dealing with the issues and concerns of employees or their interests lie exclusively in operational performance. It's like a professional football coach who truly couldn't care less about the players. The coach's enthusiasm and motivation come solely from winning games. The players (employees) soon come to resent the coach's lack of interest, caring, and commitment to them.

Start connecting with the employees. Establish techniques that allow you to interact with employees. For example, once a month, randomly select twenty employees to have lunch with in a conference room. Discuss how the company is doing and gauge how the employee population is feeling. Host small focus groups consisting of randomly selected employees. Have the facilitator discuss issues and concerns that employees may be having. Initiate teambuilding activities and continuous-improvement teams. Finally, add into the mix some social events such as potlucks or barbecues.

The "I Don't Have Time to Communicate" Manager

This represents the manager who is always too busy to see employees or provide adequate communication to the organization. For empowerment to work, it requires lots of communication. If managers aren't willing to spend the time required to effectively communicate with employees, they shouldn't engage in employee empowerment. They will make the employees anxious and may find the employees' results unsatisfactory.

Advice

If you can't find the time to communicate important information to your employees, or they complain about the lack of communication, you may require additional structure. Make communication part of your normally scheduled activities. Generate and publish a schedule for one-on-one, staff, and department meetings with employees. This will make it harder to cancel the communication sessions. Also devise short meetings on operational topics so that needed discussion occurs. Lastly, establish a culture where people can drop by your office as needed to discuss matters.

The absence of communication can occur if managers don't understand their role in a values-based, highly empowered, continuous-improvement environment. For example, rather than coaching and removing barriers for their employees, managers might spend too much time working on their own projects or being stuck in the office.

The "I Don't Have Time to Coach or Develop My Employees" Manager

This management style reflects managers who can't find the time, or won't spend the time, to grow employees. These managers often don't believe it's their job to grow the employees. You may hear them say, "I'm not a trainer." Or, "They should take a night class if they want to learn that; I'm too busy."

In some instances, such managers may be threatened by hiring or developing high performers. They operate out of a fear that as their employees become more valuable, the managers become less valuable. Therefore, they hire mediocre performers and don't spend enough time coaching them. They have no interest in developing their people because they wrongly think it would make them more vulnerable.

Advice

In today's flat organizational structures, and with the incredible demand placed on managers, it can be difficult to find time to coach employees. However, coaching and developing employees are essential tasks. Training is one of the foundational elements for maintaining a company's continuous-improvement culture. Employee development fuels the improvement activities. Real-time coaching and a strong training system create the continuous learning and adaptive employees essential for excelling in today's highly competitive marketplace.

Managers should utilize one-on-one employee meetings to coach and develop their staff. Employee development is a win-win proposition for both the employee and the employer. The employee acquires additional skills and enjoys learning new things, while the employer gains increased capabilities and enhanced productivity. Don't find time to develop your employees—make time. It's every manager's job to develop a strong organization. Employee development is imperative to achieving this objective.

The "Politics Is My Game" Manager

This represents the manager who can be characterized by a strong personality and high ego, a manager who spends too much time playing politics with rivals. This management style kills employee empowerment because it teaches employees to spend their time accumulating and wielding power rather than on making improvements and being team players. It shifts the fight from the company's competitors to each other.

Advice

If you're this type of manager, you must begin your development by looking within. You need to discover why you have these personality traits, how they have benefited you, and how they are now limiting your goals. Reflect on the values you are projecting—that spending time playing politics is more important than accomplishing the work, and that teamwork is not necessary.

You need to start seeing the world differently. You will gain even better results by distributing power, rather than accumulating it. Your pride should stem from being the best manager you've ever met. The days of the good old boys are coming to an end.

The "I Hate Change" Manager

This characterization represents the manager who fundamentally doesn't like change. This personality trait typically permeates both the manager's professional and personal life. You may hear such managers saying, "There's too much information and change in the world today." Or, "Why can't things just stay the same?" The problem this trait imposes is that in a continuous-improvement environment, it's imperative that managers embrace change, not resist it.

Advice

Try creating an increased sense of routine by incorporating change into your normal operational meetings and plans. For example, develop a basic procedure for change control. Set a forum wherein you and other managers review the status of improvement projects and ensure the employees are following the change-control procedures. In this way, you will feel a greater sense of structure and more control. Make change a routine. We also recommend that you read *Who Moved My Cheese?* by Spencer Johnson. This book provides a powerful insight to understanding how to effectively embrace change.

If you're constantly experiencing frustration or anxiety as change occurs, step back and determine if you're suited for this type of environment. Life is short; if you require more routine in your job, you may want to look elsewhere.

The "I'll Do It for You" Manager

This manager doesn't have a need to micromanage, but rather accomplishes tasks that should be completed by the employees. Such managers can't say no to employees, are uncomfortable asking employees to do things, or remove the employees' responsibilities out of pure kindness. They have lost the balance between coaching the employees and holding them accountable for fulfilling their job responsibilities.

This characterization may also describe managers who find it easier to do the task themselves. They often say, "It'll take too much time to show the employee how to do it, so I'll just do it myself." In other cases, they may find it difficult to say no when asked for assistance. The downside of this style is that it deprives the employees from carrying out assignments. The employees are then unable to grow their skills. Moreover, employee accountability and acceptance of delegated authority are fundamental to empowerment.

Advice

It's great to be a kind person. But any strength taken too far is a weakness. In the long run, you're not benefiting the employees by helping them too much because it limits their growth. For example, when an employee is to be terminated, the group's senior manager often asks who should conduct the termination. Should the senior manager do it personally, or should the employee's direct supervisor terminate the employee? When we're asked this question, it means that the senior manager is concerned about the supervisor's ability to terminate the employee in a professional manner. We advise such managers to let the direct supervisor conduct the termination and then we give the senior manager some tips on how to coach the supervisor through the termination process. If the supervisor never learns how to terminate employees professionally, you're limiting both that person's growth and career advancement. Managers and supervisors must learn how to properly terminate employees.

Often, managers who fail to hold employees accountable for their job responsibilities are over-sympathizing with the employee's situation. Step back from the situation and remember that it's the employee's obligation to meet performance standards. Provide coaching as needed, stop yourself when you're over-sympathizing with the employee's difficulty in completing the assignment, and ensure the employee performs acceptably.

Frequently this situation stems from the manager's inability to be assertive or from the need to avoid potential conflict. Here the manager must learn to confront others in a direct but professional manner. Practice being more direct with others on issues in which you know the other person will not overreact if you're being assertive. This will allow you to gain confidence and hone your ability to be more direct. Then you can build your skills further in more dicey situations.

The "It's Okay to Have Favorites" Manager

This represents the manager who clearly has favorite employees. I'm sure all managers have employees they favor over others. This management style becomes an issue when the favoritism become excessive as perceived by the other employees, or when favored employees use their status to gain power over the other employees.

Such managers say, "This employee's marginal performance or conduct is okay because he has worked for me for a long time and/or he is a friend." If the favorite employee becomes a barrier to improvement or to teamwork, the group won't bring the issue to the manager. Therefore, a whole set of issues never gets addressed.

The negative results associated with this style are amplified when the favorites are not the highest-performing employees. This is how the good old boy cultures originate. Employees' enthusiasm and commitment decrease when they see that success depends on having favorite status rather than the merit of their contributions. Employees are typically motivated by the sense of accomplishment that comes with making improvements. If that feeling is lessened because the status of employees is not associated with their level of contribution, employees' motivation will decrease.

Advice

If perceived favoritism is negatively affecting employee morale or the improvement process, you should decrease your ties to the perceived favorites. Determine what you're doing that makes the employees think a person is your favorite and then moderate that behavior. For example, are you granting certain employees more exceptions to the rules, lowering performance expectations, or always asking for their opinion in meetings? Do you frequently go to lunch with them or have them over to the house?

If you find that the perceived favorite is boasting about his or her status or relationship with you, or is using it inappropriately, tell the employee that this is unacceptable. Back away from the employee a bit to reinforce the discussion.

The "I Need to Lay Low" Manager

This represents the manager who may shortly be retiring, who is on a performance improvement plan, or who wants to avoid receiving an additional project or request. In business we refer to these individuals as short-timers.

Advice

Get in the game or get out. It's not fair to take the company's compensation and give marginal performance in return. Employees will soon discover your lack of commitment. This poor role modeling will decrease the employees' appetite for expending the extra effort required to maintain an improvement-oriented culture. Managers need to lead by example.

The "I'll Wait This Employee Empowerment Thing Out" Manager

You may hear this manager say, "There's lots of talk, but things never change around here." Or, "It's just another corporate program that will soon be forgotten, so I don't need to play the game." We can understand this person's mind-set. Since it's rare for companies to change enough in-put variables to affect the status quo, lasting change is seldom achieved. They have seen countless corporate initiatives that have been imple-mented but that subsequently fade away. They have learned that the more things change, the more they remain the same. Therefore, they have de-cided to neither accept nor reject senior management's push for employee empowerment and nonstop continuous improvement, but rather to skep-tically wait and see if they're serious this time.

Advice

If this describes your management style, you're reducing your opportunity for career advancement. The managers who stand on the sidelines are never fast-tracked. You must put your skepticism aside and try employee empowerment and continuous improvement. You'll like the results.

As Microchip's CEO, Steve recorded a videotaped message for the em-ployees. In the video Steve said, "There are three kinds of people in this world. There are the first kind, who make things happen. These are the in-dividuals who get involved, change things, and constantly keep up with the best in the world. Then there are the second kind, who watch while things are happening. These are the individuals who don't tend to get involved and always have a wait-and-see attitude. Then there are the third kind, who wonder what really happened. The formula for world-class success changes right in front of their eyes, but they can't change fast enough to keep pace. Managers need to belong to the first group: individuals who make things happen."

During our years at Microchip, and previously at Intel, we have come across numerous executives and managers fitting many of the management styles described in this chapter. The role of the CEO and Human Resources executive is to monitor, track, guide, develop, and mentor the executives to adopt the most effective management style for the particular situation. Individuals whose management style has become a barrier to optimizing the effectiveness of the organization seldom change their style without pressure from their supervisor. If the CEO has a strong style problem and is not open to feedback, he or she will most likely not change.

9

Discovering the Origins of
Behavior and Job Performance

AN INDIVIDUAL'S BEHAVIOR, expressed through job performance, represents the culmination of a series of dynamic and complex human processes. In this chapter, we'll trace behavior to its origins, examining the basic chemistry and physics of personality and behavior. An employee's job performance represents only the tip of the iceberg. There's a vast depth to employees that often remains untapped. It's trapped inside the employee by a management team and systems that restrict or neglect the employee's true potential. Management must commit to gaining the expertise and establishing systems that will yield this potential. You can optimize your employees' performance by managing them at this deeper level. In turn, this will lead to greater operational success.

If you want to gain the full benefits associated with a values-based, highly empowered, continuous-improvement culture, the potential of each employee must be realized. This requires a solid management team— a team of managers and supervisors striving to harness the power held in employee empowerment. If you want to become a stellar manager, you need a basic proficiency in people management. For some, these people skills come naturally; the rest of us acquire them through study and practice. This chapter will aid in that study.

The Necessity of People Skills

Company cultures constantly striving to improve the enterprise by empowering employees create three conditions that require excellent management skills: (1) Striving for improvement, by its very nature, pressures the *norm-state* (what people are currently accustomed to), stressing the employees. (2) Since decision-making authority is distributed throughout the organization by means of employee empowerment, the gray area in which employees operate is increased. (3) These types of cultures simply ask more of their employees. Employees are required to constantly enhance their strengths and decrease their weaknesses, requiring managers to understand the basic psychology involved in effective people management. This is typically accomplished by senior managers sharing their expertise with more junior managers and by the services provided by a training organization.

Some employees feel stimulated by the significant demands that come with empowerment and continuous improvement. They crave the challenges and variety associated with these demanding cultures. Some employees, however, feel pressured by the demand to constantly improve. One great thing about these cultures, though, is that over time most employees become accustomed to the constant changes they produce. You may hear the employees say, "Now that the big initiative is finally done, what am I going to do with my time? It doesn't feel right not working on a new improvement initiative." These employees often feel uncomfortable or unsatisfied when they're not engaged in some form of improvement activity. This discomfort with merely maintaining the status quo is one psychological factor that facilitates improvement-oriented cultures.

In contrast, under rules-based cultures, employees are primarily dealt with at the behavioral level. Therefore, only a marginal understanding of people management is necessary. Managers diligently work to ensure everyone conforms to the rules. Managers who succeed in this type of culture are people who thrive when there is an absence of a gray area, where the work setting has a right answer or procedure for practically every situation. The rules provide the structure these individuals crave, constantly leading them in the prescribed direction.

At a deeper level, a highly structured culture satisfies these individuals' excessive need for stability and security. This is one of the reasons why some people like rules-based environments. Additionally, these cultures can be more straightforward than continuous-improvement cultures because they require less intellectual understanding and demand less of the employee. Unfortunately, rules-based cultures fail to fully tap into the employees' true potential—and, therefore, the company's potential. Typically, rules-based cultures yield average results from the average employee, rather than extraordinary results, as we shall discuss in the employee performance output equation described in Chapter 19.

Discovering the Origins

The diagram illustrated in Figure 9.1 shows the four levels from which behavior originates. They are the foundation, core, application, and visible levels. Though each of these levels is built on the previous level, there is a great deal of overlap. The dynamic interaction between each level required to elicit a behavioral action can't be captured in any two-dimensional representation. Nevertheless, the chart clearly illustrates the elements that produce personality and behavior.

Figure 9.1 shows that several components interact dynamically in order to produce an observable behavior. The components from which behavior stems include one's genetics, human needs, environmental experiences, aptitudes, interests, and values. These govern the skills, knowledge, attitudes, and motivations the person acquires, eventually culminating in the employee's job performance. The following sections explain each of the components that comprise personality and behavior.

Level One—The Foundation Level: Genetics

The foundation level shown in Figure 9.1 represents the influences of genetic predisposition, basic human needs, and life experiences on shaping one's behavior. For many years, academics and researchers argued over the relative influences of genetics versus environment on the formation of personality and behavior.

The genetics camp concluded that one's genes played the dominant

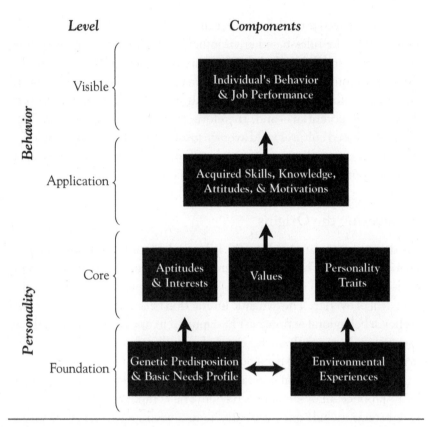

Figure 9.1: Four Levels of the Origins of Personality and Behavior

role. Their research has found that genetics do indeed play a significant role in forming personality. This research proceeded in concert with the medical field's findings that genetics play a role in one's predisposition for particular illnesses. Today, the impact of our genetics is well understood.

Parents have long recognized the relationship between genetics and personality. Anyone with children knows that each child comes into the world with a unique personality and varying abilities. There are generalized differences between the genders, and variation within each gender. A parent may find that one of his or her children demands lots of human interaction and another very little. One child may be a fighter while the next child is passive. One child may have a high need for security while the other child is a risk taker.

An individual's genetic makeup significantly influences his physical features, athletic abilities, intelligence, memory, analytical capability, and so forth. Consequently, one's genetics play an extensive role in shaping many of the other components that form personality and drive behavior. For example, if an individual is blessed with great athletic prowess, this will directly impact his or her aptitude for sports and jobs requiring physical dexterity or strength. We typically gravitate towards things that utilize our strengths and provide positive reinforcement. Therefore, an individual with such athletic aptitude may develop an interest in sports and pursue a profession related to that field.

Alternately, an individual born with a genetic predisposition for analytical reasoning would have a strong aptitude for mathematics or problem solving. This person may become interested in engineering. Nevertheless, nothing in life is predestined. Through life experience, both of these individuals could develop an interest in sociology and become psychologists or social workers. However, the influence of their aptitudes, stemming from their genetic makeup, is always at work shaping their personality and abilities.

Employees' performance and attendance can suffer due to conditions such as depression or alcoholism. Researchers have demonstrated that depression and alcoholism can stem from a genetic predisposition. This type of predisposition often runs in families, once again illustrating the relationship between genetics and personality. Employees whose performance or attendance is impacted by depression or alcoholism can be helped through medication and counseling. Supervisors should take notice of employees who are showing the signs of these types of conditions.

Employers should provide an employee assistance service programs. Such programs offer employees five or ten free visits to a mental health provider. This service allows employees to address their issues in a confidential setting. Over time, this program will more than pay for itself by improving employee productivity, attendance, and turnover.

Companies also should have a documented policy on substance abuse. This policy allows employees who are seeking assistance to come forward.

In this case, the company will provide appropriate services for the person's recovery. However, if the person is breaching the policy and doesn't come forward, this person's employment should be terminated.

Supervisors should be able to have their employees submit to alcohol and drug testing if warranted. This should be done through the Human Resources department. We recommend that employees be subjected to this type of testing only if there is reasonable cause. If you do random testing or plant narks in your workforce, it will have a negative effect on the culture and the employees' job satisfaction. Only circumstances surrounding safety or security should be cause for exception to this rule. How the company and supervisors handle these types of situations can either enhance or erode their employees' job satisfaction and the likeability of management.

Level One—The Foundation: Human Needs

The renowned psychologist and author, Abraham Maslow, described the basic needs that all people seek to satisfy. These universal human needs are referred to as Maslow's Hierarchy of Needs, which include physiological, safety and security, belonging and love, self-esteem, and self-actualization needs. He explained that first we seek to satisfy our more basic physical needs, such as those associated with hunger or warmth. We then work to satisfy our needs to feel safe and secure.

We spend much of our lives pursuing our need to belong, to love and be loved, and to gain a measure of self-esteem. Finally, we strive to satisfy our need for self-actualization—to utilize our full potential and attempt to become the person we once dreamed we could be.

Our genetics play a large role in the formation of our human needs profile. We are born with a unique profile, varying by degrees, not by absolutes. One person may have a greater need for security than another person, and so on. Nevertheless, to some degree we all need to feel safe and secure. An individual's human needs profile has a tremendous influence on the eventual formation of his or her personality, abilities, and behavior. For example, a manager who began his or her career as a production worker may have a stronger need for esteem and a lesser need for belonging than the average production worker. This manager's high need for esteem (within the workplace) drove him or her to separate from his or her peers and become a manager. The manager was willing to ignore his or her need to belong (stay with the group) in order to gain the status associated with being the leader of the group. Gaining an awareness of your employees' needs and motivations increases your managerial effectiveness and competence in providing career counseling.

Level One—The Foundation: Environmental Experiences

Since Sigmund Freud began his investigation into the human psyche in the late 1800s, theorists and researchers have tirelessly examined the influence of environmental experiences on shaping personality and behavior. In the 1950s, B. F. Skinner opened a branch of study called Behaviorism. The behaviorists claimed that environmental factors play the primary role in shaping personality and behavior. They ushered in the behavior modification movement. The essence of behavior modification is that you can shape anyone's behavior if you gain control over his or her environment. Behavior modification explains current behavioral actions as a consequence of previous behaviors being positively reinforced, negatively reinforced, or punished.

If you've ever taken Psychology 101 in college, you've seen behavior modification in action. You'll recall those endless studies of defenseless rats subjected to bizarre experiments. If the rats achieved the desired behavior, they received a treat. If they failed the task, they were exposed to an electrical shock. We'd have to admit that these experiments would surely shape our behavior, too. We'd be willing to complete all manner of bizarre tasks to avoid electrocution.

We now know that behavior modification is not a comprehensive explanation for describing the formation of personality and behavior. Even so, the behaviorists have made an invaluable contribution to the science of psychology. What's now known is that one's environmental experiences have a profound influence on shaping personality and behavior.

Parents, religious affiliations, teachers, and friends clearly help shape our values, interests, and personality traits. If a father is very competitive and loves sports, it's likely that the son will be encouraged to participate in sports and to adopt a competitive personality trait. We've all spent our Saturday mornings exposed to the father, poised at the sideline, yelling at the son, "Toughen up" or "Try harder." This unquestionably has an impact on the formation of the child's personality.

There is a well-accepted answer to the question: "Do genetics or environment have a greater impact on shaping us?" The answer is that they both play a significant, interrelated role. Moreover, personality and behavior are a result of countless real-time interactions between our physical body and our collective experiences.

Level Two—The Core: Aptitudes and Interests

An *aptitude* refers to an individual's natural mental or physical strengths or talents within a particular area. A person may have an aptitude for such things as math, writing, problem solving, verbal communication, or athletics. If you say that a person learned something easily, you're saying that this person has a natural aptitude to learn or perform that specific skill or set of skills. If an individual has the ability to quickly mimic rhythms, tempos, and musical chords, this person is likely to have an aptitude for music. Hence, this individual may want to become a musician because it's likely such a person would be good at it.

In contrast, if an individual is tone deaf and has difficulty mimicking rhythms, this person has a low aptitude for music and may have difficulty becoming a great musician. In no way does this mean that with lots of motivation and hard work this person couldn't become a good musician. It just means that this person will have to work harder at becoming a great musician than someone who has an aptitude for music.

An *interest* refers to something people like or dislike. We have a level of interest in every activity in which we engage. An individual's interest in a particular area can range from marginal to intense. People tend to engage in activities that they like and steer away from activities they don't like. Therefore, we say that someone has an interest in something if that individual seems to enjoy it. A person may have an interest in working with others, while another person may enjoy creating software.

The key to interests is obvious. Only a few individuals within the population typically will stick with a job consisting of job responsibilities they don't like. So, try to match job functions with employees' interests whenever possible. Employees understand the correlation between aptitude and interest, since they tend to gravitate toward things in which they excel and like.

It's important that you as the manager have a basic understanding of your employees' general aptitudes and interests. If an employee has little aptitude for math but can do it adequately and has a high aptitude for conceptual analysis, you should assign this person to do analysis and problem-solving tasks, rather than basic accounting, whenever possible. This is not to say that as a manager you should always avoid assigning employees tasks for which they may have limited aptitude. Only in this way can employees grow and improve their weaknesses.

Remember that interest feeds motivation. If we're interested in making more money, we're more likely to work overtime or longer hours to receive that promotion. Spend the time necessary to investigate what interests your employees. Help them clarify their short- and long-term interests and career goals. You can increase your employees' commitment and performance by giving them assignments that match their interests. They'll work harder since interest fuels motivation. If your employees get bored easily and like stimulating tasks, give them the critical, highly visible, short-term projects. If they like seeing the long-term vision, spell out a career path with long-term appeal.

Level Two—The Core: Values and Personality Traits

Values are the criteria we use to judge and evaluate our own behaviors and those of others. They are the filters through which we place value on the things within our world. Moreover, values, like personality traits, drive our decisions and actions. For example, a soldier goes off to war because of the value placed on country. A minister consoles others because of the value placed on mankind. The outstanding sales clerk provides excellent customer service because of the value placed on satisfying others. Every employer wants to hire individuals who value working hard. They also want to hire people whose values complement those practiced by the company.

Since much of our behavior is driven by our values, its importance can't be overstated. When Steve was watching the television show *Cops*, this truth became self-evident. On the one hand, you see the values of the criminal mind. Criminals clearly feel they have a legitimate right to take other people's property. On the other hand, you see the police officers risking their lives, guided by the value of protecting others and maintaining order. The only true difference between these two groups of citizens is their fundamental set of values. One set of values will drive a lifetime of crime, while the other set will drive a lifetime of service to others.

You can maximize your employees' performance by understanding the role that values play in driving job performance. Your employees' values may be the most important asset of your business. For example, an employee who values others will be a good team player. Employees who value company profits will keep down expenses, and so on. In a values-based, highly empowered, continuous-improvement culture, it's essential that your employees' values mimic those of the company. If they don't, the culture you desire will never be realized.

Personality traits are those fundamental and lasting traits or characteristics people use to describe one's personality. Honest, stable, considerate, conscientious, outgoing, communicative, controlling, shy, quiet, adaptable, achievement-oriented, assertive, passive, persistent, organized, caring, or nervous are examples of personality traits. These traits are formed through a combination of one's genetic makeup and environmental experiences. This entire chapter concentrates on becoming a more effective manager through managing employees at a deeper level. Addressing an employee's personality trait that is impeding that person's potential performance represents one of these deeper levels of managing.

An employee's personality traits are one of the major components that continually drive an employee's skill level and job performance. Every day, countless behaviors stem from any single trait. Therefore, mastering the ability to address, at the trait level, areas that are limiting the employee's potential success has a tremendous multiplying effect. By positively affecting even one personality trait, the manager may enhance hundreds of future decisions and actions without any further intervention.

An employee we'll call Russ Kite, whom Michael managed for just over a year, exemplifies how addressing a personality trait, rather than a behavior, can yield great results. In a one-on-one setting, Russ had no trouble commenting on or giving feedback about how to improve things. In fact, he was quite outspoken. He had excellent and well-thought-out opinions on most of the issues and challenges facing the organization. However, Russ never spoke in meetings—he gave no input and no feedback.

Russ made a habit of stopping by Michael's office prior to every critical meeting. After his ritualistic opening comment, "Well, I was just in the neighborhood," followed by his overused transition line, "So, what's new?" the conversation inevitability drifted to the items on the meeting's agenda. Russ would enthusiastically express his opinions to Michael on each of the agenda topics. His views were worthy of discussion. So, Michael would tell Russ, "That sounds great. You should suggest that at the meeting!" Michael always noticed a lull in Russ's enthusiasm when he made the suggestion. Russ would glance out the office window, murmuring, "Oh, maybe I should." But based on his past behavior and how his voice inflection trailed off as he said, "Maybe I should," it was apparent he wouldn't.

As usual, Michael was forced to make Russ's points and fight his battles for him at the meeting. Russ was senior enough that he should have expressed his own views and fought his own battles. Michael decided that this game would cease. One way or another, Russ was going to stand on his own.

On several occasions Michael addressed this issue with Russ. He would express his disappointment, telling Russ that he expected him to speak up from now on. But things never changed. Over time Michael would get angrier with Russ, and Russ would become more aloof when the topic was discussed. A new course of action was warranted.

Michael realized that he had been dealing with Russ at the behavioral level, telling Russ his expectations and expressing his disappointment with Russ's inability to meet them. Michael concluded that a more sophisticated approach was essential. He would delve deeper into what was causing Russ to avoid speaking up at meetings. And this time Michael would not be appeased by Russ's usual reply: "Well, I guess I'll just have to start speaking up more."

The first thing Michael realized was that he couldn't address the issue in a fashion that made Russ defensive. This would cause Russ to shut down and begin to defend his actions. They'd already played that game. No, Michael needed to adopt an approach, and maintain a demeanor, that opened Russ up to honestly addressing the issues. Michael wanted to help

Russ uncover the origin of this apprehension toward public speaking. Further, Michael wanted Russ, on a very personal level, to acquire the desire to overcome this obstacle. Russ needed to internalize the negative effects this condition was having on his current and future success as a manager.

Michael asked Russ to come by the office at 2:30 P.M. Anticipating that maybe there was trouble, Russ arrived promptly. Russ sat in his usual chair, the one across the desk, on the right. He initiated the conversation, asking, "Well, what's up?" Michael replied, "I know we've discussed this before, but I need you to speak up more in the meetings." Russ responded, "I know."

Michael then stated, "In yesterday's meeting, I had to make your points for you again. I'm sorry, Russ, but this time things must change. You're a senior manager and it's your job to speak up in meetings. This is a condition of your employment. I can't have managers who won't communicate in a group setting! Most of the decisions we make around here happen in meetings. In addition to hurting your current performance, it'll impede any further promotional opportunities." Russ paused, then said, "I understand."

"Have you ever thought about why you're so apprehensive about speaking up?" Michael asked. "Russ, you're a great guy, and I'm a hundred percent behind you. You know that!" he said, in an attempt to make Russ feel more at ease. "Does this issue affect you outside of work?" "Sure," Russ replied. "This is obviously a personality trait you've acquired along the way," Michael said softly. "Do you know where it comes from?"

"Well, I think it's from when I was in grade school. You see, I've never been a good speaker. I know what I want to say, but when I go to say it, I lose my point. I remember that in the eighth grade I had to give an oral book report to the class. I made my notes and my mother had me practice my presentation three times. When I presented my book report to the class, it was a disaster," he shared in a voice that seemed quite vulnerable. "I got all mixed up. Starting, then fidgeting, then restarting, and so on. I could hear the kids laughing. I needed to run, run anywhere; somewhere I could hide from everyone. But I couldn't. So I pushed on, and the kids' laughter just got louder."

Russ continued, "Finally, midway through the presentation, my teacher, Miss Lang, said, 'Russ, thank you, that was very nice. You can take your seat now.' I was relieved, but as I made that long walk back to my desk, her act of mercy made me feel even more humiliated. I realized that I was so bad she wouldn't even let me finish! At recess the humiliation persisted: the normal teasing you'd expect from the other kids after such a public spectacle. This happened to me on several other occasions. So I made a pact with myself to never speak in public again. It's just not worth it."

Michael said, "Russ, a lot has changed since the eighth grade. Are you going to let this traumatic episode govern the rest of your life? Is this unproductive trait going to continue to limit your effectiveness as a manager? Will it halt your career growth? I know you can fix this. Are you willing to commit to improving the situation?"

"I'm not sure where to start. If I could have fixed this problem, I would have done it a long time ago," Russ said with deep introspection.

"Well, let's develop a course of action that is do-able," Michael commented. "Let's start small so you can build up your confidence," he suggested. Russ nodded.

Russ and Michael worked together in establishing a plan of action. The plan initially involved speaking up on one small point per meeting. This process would continue to build until Russ could give a twenty-minute presentation at the monthly staff meeting. Michael and Russ's mutual goal was for Russ to achieve this in three months. In addition, Russ would utilize a technique to keep his anxiety down while communicating in a group setting. He would pretend that everyone in the room worked for him. Consequently, the "audience" became less threatening.

Russ's progress was amazing. Since he had "internalized" the issue and took full ownership for decreasing the influence of this unwelcome personality trait, things began to change. Russ had his ups and downs, but achieved the three-month goal. It's unlikely that Russ will ever become a great public speaker. However, Michael was pleased with, and proud of, his progress. Two other side benefits occurred. The decision to manage Russ at a deeper level strengthened their working relationship and increased Russ's loyalty. Michael guessed Russ appreciated the approach and the opportunity to improve himself. In addition, Russ began to vocalize his positions in meetings outside the organization. Other vice presidents began commenting on the value of Russ's insights.

As we've said, by positively affecting just one personality trait, you'll enhance hundreds of future decisions and actions. In this case, a door to a lifetime of new career opportunities was also opened for Russ. Chapter 11 provides managers with tools and methods to manage employees at the value or trait level.

Hiring People with the Desired Trait-Sets and Values

When interviewing prospective candidates, we're not only assessing their educational background, work experience, and accomplishments, but we're also trying to gain insight into their personality. We're trying to answer complex questions such as: Who is this person? What is she like? What drives him? We attempt to shed light on those predictive questions. Will the candidate be a good performer, a dependable employee, and a diligent worker? Will he thrive in the company's culture? Will she be effective, given her supervisor's management style? Are his career aspirations compatible with the opportunities available within the organization? The answer to these sorts of questions lies in the candidate's personality traits and values. Supervisors who can assess these softer aspects of the candidate's personality make better hiring decisions.

Make a concerted effort to hire candidates whose personality traits and values match the company's culture and the job responsibilities. In addition to establishing the standard selection criteria, such as education and work history, define the desired *trait-set*—those specific traits indicative of success—that you're seeking for that specific position.

Figure 9.2 illustrates an example of a desired trait-set for a Field Sales Engineer position. It shows the desirable set of traits and the degree to which the various traits are utilized in this position. For example, persuasiveness is used 90% of the time while the engineer is on a sales call. Persistence is required 90% of the time, listening 70%, and so forth. Convert these requirements into a tool to be utilized during the interviewing process.

Figure 9.3 is an example of such a tool. Each interviewer should complete the assessment tool after the interview. This assessment, combined with the team's overall assessment, should aid in selecting the best candidate. Anyone who interviews candidates should receive training about discrimination. Care must be taken to ensure your assessment tools, and the

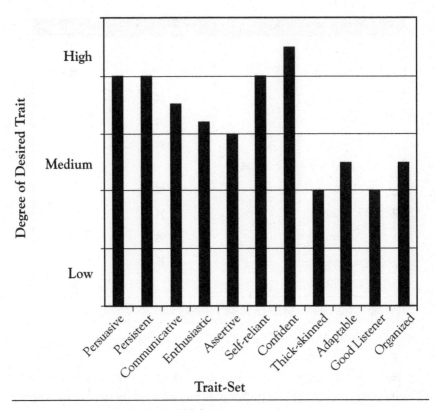

FIGURE 9.2: Desired *Trait-Set* for Field Sales Engineer

other interviewers, never purposely or accidentally utilize any approach or tool that could be construed as discriminatory in nature.

Level Three—Application: Acquired Skills, Knowledge, Attitudes, and Motivation

You don't become who you are by accident. Your personality represents the culmination of all the components, specific to you, laid out in Figure 9.1. If we could trace the totality of your origins, given a specific situation, your attitudes and actions could be predicted with relative accuracy. We could even make some good predictions on the types of occupations you may pursue and the likelihood of your success.

Trait-Set	Too Little	Just Right	Too Much
Persuasive		✖	
Persistent			✖
Communicative		✖	
Enthusiastic		✖	
Assertive		✖	
Self-reliant	✖		
Confident		✖	
Thick-skinned		✖	
Adaptable		✖	
Good Listener		✖	
Organized			✖

Overall Assessment: Meets *trait-set* requirements

FIGURE 9.3: *Trait-Set* Assessment Tool Used for Field Sales Engineer Candidate

These predictions can never be a certainty because each of us is still a work in progress. Our personalities may be modified by significant experiences yet to arrive, sudden crises, or just the natural maturing process. These experiences may alter our underlying values, interests, and traits. This, in turn, may lead us to set new priorities or pursue new dreams. We've all heard of the physician who quit his prestigious practice to serve as a missionary or as a crusader for some worthy cause.

As with your personality, the skills, knowledge, attitudes, and motivations that you acquire are driven from the components shown in Figure 9.1. You don't choose to be a plumber, farmer, businessman, doctor, rodeo rider, politician, or professional golfer by accident, though it may appear that way at first glance. Rather, with careful study, you can uncover how your aptitudes, interests, values, and personality traits influenced your choice of occupation and your level of success.

You may be asking, "What role does pure 'chance' play in predicting someone's success?" During our lives, various opportunities (luck) are presented to each of us. These chance events do add some randomness to the equation, but you still choose to pursue or ignore specific opportunities. How many opportunities that you never even saw or opted not to pursue have come along? For example, take that summer job working at the Shell gas station on Elm Street, the one you passed up in high school because you wanted to hang out with the guys. Who knows? Maybe you would have become a mechanic after a few summers. You might have liked it so much that you worked to purchase the station from old, cranky Mr. Chaney, rather than pursuing college. Maybe this experience would have given you a true hunger to complete an advanced college degree so you could work with your mind versus your body; nobody will ever know—nobody even cares.

We do know that your decision to hang out with the guys rather than accepting the job was a direct result of the culmination and interplay of your aptitudes, interests, values, personality traits, and parents. Both you and your parents valued your free time more than what you might have gained from the experience—learning responsibility, working hard, and earning a portion of your own money.

We're not saying that choosing not to take the job was the right or wrong decision. We just want you to see how your decision to decline the job was a result of your parents and you acting on each of your unique personalities. Virtually thousands of opportunities are presented to us through life's twists and turns. The decisions we make, and the efforts we expend chasing opportunities, are driven by the unique origins of our personality.

Our personality even affects what we choose to study in college. In college, countless students Steve knew were undecided on which major they should pursue. Over a lunch they'd comment, "My parents think I should study business or political science. They think I'd make a good lawyer and lawyers make a lot of money, you know!" Steve would ask, "Well, what do you want to be?" The standard reply was, "I'm not sure." When a senior gave this answer, Steve knew he or she was going to be a low achiever.

Steve noticed that most of his friends selected a field they found interesting, played to their strengths, or served as a prerequisite for future career aspirations. But what these motivators all had in common was that they reflected the students' values, though they had never given it enough thought to draw this conclusion. As you're aware, male college students are not revered for their introspection. Their focus is more immediate. "Who has the beer?" "How do I meet girls?" And, most pressing, "How am I going to pass this afternoon's test, which I haven't studied for?" Steve found that if the student was interested in, and valued, understanding more about him- or herself, he or she ended up majoring in psychology. If he or she was interested in material things, and valued money, he or she often selected a business track. If animals or nature were highly valued, he or she studied biology, and so on. The students' aptitudes, interests, values, and personality traits, more than chance, directed their path. These four aspects drove the expertise the students acquired in college.

Level Four—The Visible Level: Behavior and Job Performance

We've discussed the benefits of managing employees at a deeper level for greater results. Yet that approach is contingent on managers first mastering the ability to effectively manage their employees at the visible level. The visible level, as shown in Figure 9.1, represents the employee's job performance that can be seen and measured. An employee's job performance is driven from factors that lie deeper within that person's psyche. The visible level is where managers spend the majority of their time managing employees. It's where expectations, standards, objectives, and goals are set and where performance indicators are established to track and measure an employee's effectiveness. Strong managers are always proficient at managing employees at this level. The outstanding people managers have also mastered the other levels (outlined in this chapter) at which employees can be managed.

An employee's performance can be measured quantitatively or qualitatively. *Quantitative measures* are those associated with objective measurements. How many widgets the employee produced per hour, the number of widgets someone ruined, or the number of days an employee was absent in a quarter are simple quantitative measurements. More complex forms of these measurements are meeting published schedules, staying within budget, and the number of new sales orders produced.

Qualitative measures are evaluations of the employee that are more subjective in nature. A supervisor's opinion on how the employee is performing is an example of a qualitative measure. Often we attempt to make qualitative measures feel more quantitative. The employee's performance appraisal is a great example. For most professional jobs, performance appraisals are based on qualitative assessments: the supervisor's conclusions on how the employee is doing, a relative assessment of the employee's output, quality, teamwork, customer service, and so forth. In order to make the supervisor's judgments appear more quantitative, we utilize formal scales. The supervisor will indicate the quality of the employee's customer service on a scale from one to ten.

Trying to make assessments of humans more structured is great. We strongly recommend this approach. However, let's not lose sight of the fact that the vast majority of assessments we make about employees are qualitative. There is nothing inherently wrong with this, but it provides another reason why we need strong managers with good judgment.

Discussions concerning an employee's performance should always begin at the visible level. The more you can quantify issues, the easier it will be for the employee to agree on the legitimacy of the problem. We think that this is self-evident. The message of this chapter is that managers should not stop here. They should utilize their "people management" skills to resolve issues early on and to unleash their employees' full potential.

10

The Weakness Principle

AN ABUNDANCE OF LITERATURE on professional and personal development is readily available. The primary thesis articulated in such literature centers on encouraging individuals to develop strengths that will either make them more valuable to the enterprise or happier people. The standard approach that these authors follow is to determine where your interests and abilities lie and to continually enhance those abilities. This is a sound tactic. When you're pursuing any career path, the journey always begins with gaining a basic competence in the field of endeavor.

What's seldom discussed in the literature is the profound role and impact your weaknesses play in limiting your success and derailing your career aspirations. This chapter is dedicated to highlighting the impact of employees' weaknesses on their ultimate success. The information is relevant to everyone from factory workers to vice presidents.

It's quite common to see employees leveraging their strengths to achieve their career aspirations. Their strengths are the upward force that drives or advances their career up through the corporate hierarchy. However, if your strategy is to enhance your strengths to advance your career, you're addressing only half of the success equation. The lesser-known portion of the equation for success centers on eliminating your weaknesses. Your weaknesses represent the downward force that constantly acts to slow your career progression. Consequently, the downward force generated by your weaknesses eventually limits your opportunity to advance.

In fact, when management determines an employee's weaknesses are greater than the strengths, that employee is often terminated. The profound impact employees' weaknesses have on their eventual success has led to the formation of *the weakness principle*. The weakness principle states that as employees progress upward through the company hierarchy, it is their weaknesses that ultimately limit success and stall their career. This occurs when the upward and downward forces created by an employee's strengths and weaknesses reach equilibrium.

Strengths Are in the Eye of the Beholder

A *strength* is a skill or an aspect of one's personality that is valued within a specific environment. A *weakness* is a lack of skill or an aspect of one's personality that is viewed unfavorably within a specific environment. Strengths and weaknesses are specific to environments and situations. They are based on the judging group's values and norms. An individual's strength in one environment may be a weakness in another. For example, one company's culture may place immense value on an individual's ability to get results at any costs, even if that means that employees alienate themselves and over time reduce the company's practice of teamwork. All that really matters are the results! In contrast, a second company may place value on obtaining results. However, the company also places value on the manner in which the result is achieved. This company may feel that, in the long run, the company will benefit from an employee population that works together.

Strengths and Weaknesses Are Job Specific

Valuing a person's specific personality traits or abilities is subjective, and depends on the job responsibilities associated with that position. A perceived strength in one job will be considered a weakness in another position, even within the same company. For example, being blunt, thick-skinned, and relentless are advantageous personality traits for collecting overdue monies. These same strengths would be considered weaknesses for a marketing manager.

The Career Stall-Point

As illustrated in Figure 10.1, an employee's career advancement stalls when equilibrium is reached between the employee's strengths and weaknesses, as perceived by the judging group. Employees' jobs become vulnerable when their undesirable personality traits and marginal performance are more prevalent than the perceived value they are adding to the operation. The manager may or may not terminate employees based on the specifics of the situation. If the manager already has a replacement candidate in mind, or has lost his or her tolerance, the employee is likely to be terminated. However, if these conditions are not present, the result will be continued employment without the opportunity for advancement. In this case, the employee has reached the career stall-point.

The more senior the position, the more an employee's weaknesses come into play. Our experience indicates that the vast majority of senior managers in corporate America are highly competent. Typically, they reach their career stall-point based on consequences related to perceived undesirable personality traits. The more senior the position, the greater influence the manager's personality has on operational performance, employees' motivation, and employees' job satisfaction. Therefore, the impact of your weaknesses increases in proportion to the level of responsibilities associated with the position.

Why Vice Presidents Don't Become CEOs

It is extremely difficult to become a first-rate CEO of a publicly held company. The position demands a remarkable scope and depth of competence, not to mention the tremendous sacrifice to your personal and family life. Normally, several highly competent vice presidents are waiting in the wings for a shot at running the enterprise. So, why will one obtain the position while the others remain vice presidents? We found this question

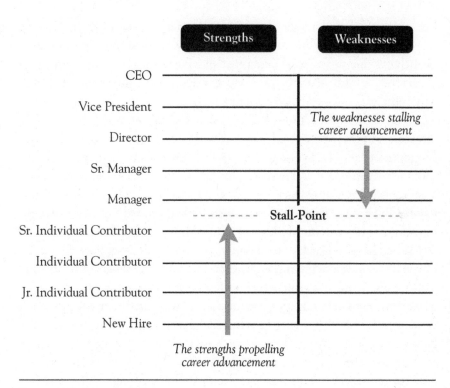

FIGURE 10.1: Career Stall-Point

intriguing from a psychological standpoint. In pursuing the answer, we formulated the weakness principle.

Many vice presidents possess incredible strengths and are quick studies. So, strengths alone can't be the decisive factor in their potential rise to CEO. Part of the answer lies in their perceived weaknesses. Moreover, the perceived weaknesses often stem from a dominant personality trait that is playing itself out. Some of the personality-related reasons for why the other vice presidents might not be selected as the new CEO include being a poor team player, a big spender, too rigid, too controlling (micromanager), too arrogant, too confrontational, too reactionary, too much of a risk taker, not liking to communicate, not being adaptable enough, having too big an ego, and not listening.

On many occasions vice presidents fail to advance due to a lack of critical expertise. For instance, they may lack an adequate understanding of sales, engineering, or manufacturing. However, it's interesting how frequently it's due to the weakness principle. For example, at a professional conference, a CEO of a software company described a situation to Steve in which the weakness principle was in effect.

Over dinner, the CEO told Steve that he had informed the board of directors and the employees that he would be retiring next year. His Vice President of Sales had gone to various board members suggesting that he should be the next CEO. He touted his many years of experience in the industry, his outstanding track record, and his robust understanding of the market and competitors. The board members agreed with these assertions. However, none of them would vote to elect him to the CEO position.

When he asked each of the board members for their support, they gave him evasive and noncommittal answers. The board members were uncomfortable discussing with him why they felt he wasn't suited for the position. They wanted to avoid the confrontation that was sure to arise if they conveyed why he wasn't going to be selected. The board members were apprehensive discussing his weaknesses with him. In fact, that symbolized part of the rationale for not promoting him. He was too confrontational and didn't listen to the inputs and feedback of others. Moreover, he wasn't a team player and the other vice presidents said they wouldn't work for him. In addition, he had on occasion taken inappropriate risks, which had hurt the sales organization.

Figure 10.2 illustrates the career stall-point of the Vice President of Sales. He had reached equilibrium between the opposing forces generated by his strengths and weaknesses. His strengths made him a first-rate Vice President of Sales, but his weaknesses would have made him a marginal CEO. He would not be a viable candidate for CEO until he reduced these weaknesses, no matter how great a Vice President of Sales he became.

Strength Profiles of High Performers

When you're evaluating the characteristics of employees who are top performers, it's beneficial to begin the analysis by discussing their *strength profile*. The profile is useful in categorizing an employee's overall strengths

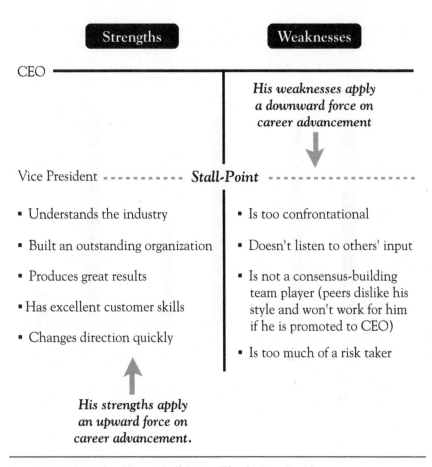

FIGURE 10.2: Example of Career Stall-Point: Why the Vice President of Sales Did Not Become CEO

and weaknesses. Figure 10.3 shows the three basic profiles of high performers. The ideal profile is that of an employee with strong strengths and low weaknesses. However, this profile is truly rare. If employees could maintain this profile as their careers advanced, they'd never experience the weakness principle. A more frequent profile is where the employee has strong strengths and medium weaknesses. Here, not only does the employee possess strong strengths, but perceived weaknesses seldom get in the

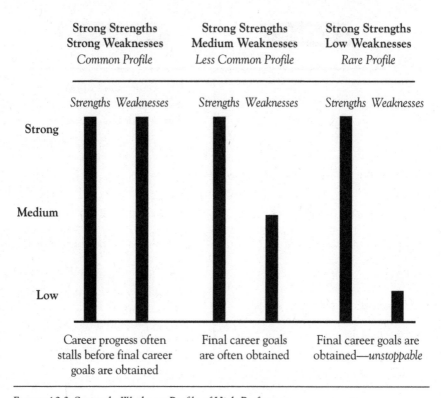

FIGURE 10.3: Strength–Weakness Profile of High Performers

way. If the employee can maintain this profile as responsibilities increase, the probability of continued success is high.

Unquestionably, many successful individuals have a strong-strengths, strong-weaknesses profile. This, by far, is the most common profile for high performers. Eventually the careers of such high performers are limited by the weakness principle. Most high performers are driven to expand their strengths while consistently achieving excellence. This profile works well if the weaknesses don't significantly impact the operational success or employees' morale. The reasons why this profile is the most common among high achievers can be found in their childhoods.

We believe that many highly successful individuals are driven by personality traits that were formed in childhood. The most common motivators are fear, competitiveness, the need to be in control, the need to lead others, and/or the need for recognition and status. Such individuals may be overcompensating for a perceived weakness, or traumatic occurrence, during childhood. They may also be attempting to avoid duplicating the conditions they associate with childhood. The key to managing employees with this common profile is to fully utilize their strengths while implementing approaches to soften or reduce the impact of their weaknesses.

Every Strength Taken Too Far Becomes a Weakness

When studying high performers with the most common strength profile—strong strengths and strong weaknesses—we discovered a fascinating thing. Frequently, such individuals' perceived weaknesses occurred when they "over-applied" their strengths. We recall a manager who did a terrific job building a highly performing organization. Initially, this manager's ability to organize and gain control over the operation was perceived as remarkable.

However, over time, employees began complaining about this manager's management style—specifically, the manager's need to micromanage everything and everyone. Ultimately, the employees lost their motivation to make improvements. Since everything had to go through the manager for approval, the bureaucracy became intolerable. Then the bureaucracy had a sweeping secondary effect. The operation's rate of improvement drastically slowed. The manager was the bottleneck at the center of this bureaucracy. The manager was taking weeks, even months, to approve proposals. The employees lost their enthusiasm, and their commitment lessened.

The manager turned his strength (his ability to organize and to control) into a weakness by micromanaging the organization. He couldn't strike a balance between his strengths and the needs of the employees. Therefore, his strength became a weakness.

It's like employees whose greatest strength is assertiveness, but who use assertiveness to resolve every situation. It's not long before no one wants to work with such people. It seems like assertiveness is the only tool in their tool bag. The over-assertiveness acts like a hammer. They try using the hammer to fix every situation, even if it's a glass window. In this case, a more sophisticated bag of tools would be beneficial. Employees with strong strengths and strong weaknesses should focus on reducing their weaknesses. The greater the employee's scope of strengths, and the fewer weaknesses, the greater success that employee will attain.

Why Work on Weaknesses versus Improving Strengths?

This is a commonly asked question. If the weakness principle is affecting your success, improving your current set of strengths may be of little benefit. If your weaknesses are limiting your performance and career progression, you need to address them. Remember, you don't necessarily have to eliminate your weaknesses to achieve additional success—reducing the weaknesses to an acceptable level may be enough. At a minimum, you should get the weaknesses off the radar screen.

Overcoming Your Weaknesses

Another commonly asked question is, "Why don't most people eliminate their weaknesses?" You don't have to be an expert to answer this question. We don't like to work on eliminating our weaknesses because it's hard work. First, many weaknesses are rooted in our personalities, which make them difficult to overcome. Second, the weakness may involve a skill deficit that would require several years of committed effort to overcome. For example, earning a college degree in electrical engineering to improve one's salary and job security is considerably more difficult than just complaining about the current situation.

Sometimes the stigmas of society prevent us from utilizing the services needed to overcome the weakness. Frequently, employees could benefit from seeking professional counseling to eliminate or control an undesirable personality trait or style of management. The problem here is obvious—in our culture, many people consider seeking counseling embarrassing, especially for people in positions of status.

The Weakness Overcome Becomes a Weakness Again

When overcoming weaknesses, be careful not to create a new one. Olympic history is full of stories of athletes overcoming childhood disabilities. Some of these athletes then pushed their bodies so far they induced life-altering injuries. We commonly read of great businessmen who came from poverty. This poverty produced a profound deep-seated fear of being poor. Even with their great wealth, these businessmen or women remain excessively frugal, trapped by fear. Therefore, work to ensure you're not overcoming one weakness while replacing it with a new one.

As described in this chapter, the weaknesses of executives, not their strengths, usually keep them from advancing further. Therefore, the CEO and the Human Resources executives must understand the strengths and weaknesses profile of the firm's various executives. Utilize feedback from the executives' peers, employees, supervisor, and so forth (i.e., the 360 degrees process) to evaluate their strengths and weaknesses. Then construct a plan to improve their weaknesses to at least an acceptable level. You'll find that executives with strong strengths and strong weaknesses recognize their strengths, but rarely see and agree with your assessment of their weaknesses. Committing to seeing your weaknesses and reducing them paves the path for further advancement.

The Human Change Process

If the Aggregate System is working, improvements will constantly introduce change. In a values-based, highly empowered, continuous-improvement culture, this means employees are required to adapt to these changing conditions and steadily enhance their own abilities. Clearly, individuals who can adapt and improve, over time, will yield higher output. The employees and managers are the firm's front-line soldiers in the quest for excellence. If you don't learn how to optimize this aspect of the *Aggregate System*, it will limit your potential success.

The Human Change Process

The *human change process* is a method for managers to increase their employees' ability to adapt and perform. This is one of the key methods for managing employees at a deeper level, as discussed in previous chapters. Today, developing employees is more than telling them what to correct and sending them to a training class. Employees need to be actively coached utilizing the human change process. Real-time coaching accelerates employees' ability to adapt and perform.

The benefits associated with real-time coaching are apparent in the field of sports. Professional sports in America is an intensely competitive industry. Teams don't just send players to training classes; instead, they employ assistant coaches to provide individualized assistance to players. As U.S. companies face stiffer international competition, the need to optimize employees' performance increases. Therefore, as with the sports industry, businesses will benefit by providing more individualized coaching.

In most instances, the employee's manager should provide the coaching. If the manager cannot do so, a mentor from outside the group can be assigned, or the employee can work with a Human Resources professional. One word of advice to manager-coaches: not all employee issues can be or should be worked on. Knowing when not to intervene is as critical as knowing when to intervene. If you get it wrong, you can make things worse.

The Components

The various components that constitute the human change process are shown in Figure 11.1. The figure illustrates the courses of action employees may take if they aren't performing or are resisting change. The manager's objective is to coach employees so that they take ownership of the issue at hand and make the needed improvement. However, employees can fall short of this objective by taking less desirable courses of action.

Employees can refuse to acknowledge the issue. They may conclude,

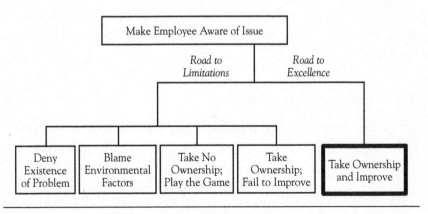

FIGURE 11.1: The Human Change Process

"The manager doesn't know what he's talking about." Employees can get stuck blaming others, saying things like, "It's someone else's fault. It's the company's fault," and so forth. Employees may pretend they're taking ownership of the issue, even when they don't believe the issue is real. They say to themselves, "This issue is not true or it's ridiculous, but I'll play their game because I'm powerless or don't want any more trouble." Finally, employees can take ownership of the issue but are incapable of improving the situation. They can be heard saying, "It's true I do have this issue. I've tried to fix it, but I just can't do it."

Gaining an Awareness of the Issue

As shown in Figure 11.1, the human change process begins by the employee gaining awareness that a problem or issue exists. This is not as straightforward as it appears. Have you ever seen employees who have no clue that their manager or coworkers are having issues with them? Issues can include performance, teamwork, problem solving, technical expertise, project management, communication, adaptability, leadership, interpersonal skills, time management, organization, and conduct. On several occasions we've seen employees deny the presence of issues even after their manager has discussed it with them. An employee may be heard saying, "My manager, or those coworkers, may have an issue with me, but they don't know what they're talking about." We have all witnessed the alcoholic who tells his spouse, "I don't have a drinking problem," and believes it.

Blaming Environmental Factors

At this stage employees readily blame any and all environmental factors for issues related to them. They're blaming the circumstances, other people, or the system for causing their issue. Such employees can be heard saying, "It's everyone else's fault." If employees remain stuck in this stage, they'll fail to make any improvement. When employees are confronted with an issue, it's natural for them to first blame the environmental factors that are contributing to the situation. So, take the time to let employees sound off.

However, keep redirecting the employees back to how they're contributing to the issue. You can accomplish this by using disarming statements such as, "I agree that some of the other technicians can be overly sensitive," or "The customer can be a pain."

Then coach employees to take some level of ownership of the issue. A manager may ask, "Setting aside for a moment that the customer can be a pain, how might you be contributing to the issue? What can you do better to improve the situation?" The manager's objective is to get the employee to take ownership for how the employee is contributing to the situation. From this stage, the employee has three separate courses of action: (1) take no ownership of the issue and just play along with management's request, (2) take ownership of the issue but fail to improve, and (3) take ownership of the issue and make the desired improvements.

Taking No Ownership; Just Playing the Game

In this stage, employees give the appearance of taking ownership of the issue. However, they're just telling management and coworkers what they want to hear. They haven't taken ownership of the issue, nor do they have a desire to change. They're just playing the game until the circumstances change. The result is a perceived change, not a real one. When the environmental forces that are driving the behavior modification cease, such employees rapidly revert to their old ways, giving up on the improvement plan.

This is not a desirable stage in which to maintain employees. However, sometimes after a concerted effort, you no longer care if employees get it or not. You just want them to perform according to expectations. If that means they're just playing a game, so be it. At least they're not causing an issue or serving as an anti-role model to the company's culture, though it may only appear that way on the surface.

The major disadvantage associated with this stage is that you don't get the benefit of employees owning up to the issue. Therefore, you'll never unleash such employees' self-perpetuating internal drive to improve. The employees, and you, have failed to tap into their true potential. Since the employees act accordingly only when the environmental force is applied, they require constant monitoring to ensure compliance. This is one of the reasons low performers take so much managerial maintenance.

The results one can expect from employees stuck in this stage are as follows:

- There is no lasting improvement.
- The employee still blames the environmental factors, but hides it from others.
- When environmental pressures subside, the employee will revert to his or her old behavior.
- In time, others will realize the employee is just playing the game.
- The employee tires of playing the game and acts out (e.g., becomes temperamental or depressed, starts being absent from work, turns to self-medication).

Taking Ownership; Failing to Improve

In this stage, the employees truly accept ownership of the issue and have an internal desire to improve. However, the improvement is never realized. For whatever reasons the employees just can't make the change. They may find that they lack the motivation, confidence, or ability to make the improvement. How many of us have been unsuccessful in our earnest attempts to lose weight, exercise more, stop worrying, quit drinking alcohol, be more assertive, spend more time with the children, communicate more effectively, or enhance our technical expertise? Let's face it, change is often extremely difficult and requires a great deal of work.

Even if employees are experiencing difficulty in realizing the desired improvement, many benefits are associated with this stage. Employees who have progressed to this stage know their issues and don't spend their time defending themselves, blaming others, or playing games. They are also more receptive to techniques that may improve the situation. They will be easier to coach in the future than those who just play the game.

The eventual results one can expect from employees stuck in this stage are as follows:

- The employee learns more about him- or herself.
- The employee matures as a person.
- The employee has positioned him- or herself for future improvements.
- Others will appreciate the employee's attempts to improve.
- The employee may have a decreased self-image.
- The employee may become discouraged.

Taking Ownership and Improving

This is the stage where employees embrace the desired improvements. They set about adapting, taking action, and growing. They say, "I own this issue and I'm going to improve." They have no difficulty comprehending how they have contributed to the situation. Employees in this stage are marked by a true desire to change. Employees with this type of attitude and commitment will discover their potential and will rise rapidly within the organization.

At this stage, the manager has two major responsibilities. First, the manager must help employees gain an insight into how the improvement will benefit their performance, increase their value to the organization, and enhance their career opportunities. Second, the manager should assist employees in establishing a development plan that outlines what changes are to be made, how they will be accomplished, and the timing. It's imperative that the manager make the development plan realistic. Don't increase the probability of failure by establishing an overly aggressive plan. Finally, whenever possible, the manager or the employee should document the plan.

The eventual results one can expect from employees in this stage are as follows:

- The employee realizes lasting improvements.
- The employee has promotional and career opportunities.
- The employee has an improved self-image.
- The employee matures and becomes a better person.
- Aspects of the employee's personal life may improve.

- Others will view the employee as successful because the employee overcame a weakness or learned something new.

Why Do People Change?

With all this talk about change it's important to spend a little time describing why people change. If managers are going to be agents of change, they need a basic understanding of why change is accepted or resisted by employees. This knowledge, combined with management's common sense, will allow management to anticipate employees' reactions. Then management can construct strategies to effectively deal with the anticipated reaction.

If management concluded that the employees would embrace a change, the strategy is to make sure the change is highlighted to employees. If a change is expected to receive mixed acceptance, the strategy is to highlight the positives and discuss the negatives. If a change will get a poor reception, the strategy is to explain in detail why the change is necessary, how it will help the company overall, and how it will be beneficial to employees in the long run. Make sure you let the employees know that the decision was difficult to make and that you do understand its ramifications on employees' lives.

Another scenario where it's useful to know why people change is when you're designing your compensation and recognition systems. Knowing what drives change in people will help you design systems that motivate employees. Finally, when you're providing individual coaching, it's essential to know what kinds of changes the individual will embrace or resist.

The following factors motivate employees to change:

- A reaction to a crisis.
- A heartfelt internal desire to change.
- A strong reward.
- The avoidance of adverse situations.
- The natural process of changing slowly over time, resulting from life's experiences and gained maturity (often occurs almost unconsciously).

- The environmental pressures ranging from an individual's spouse, child, parent, or boss, to other conditions surrounding one's physical environment.
- A reaction to mental or physical trauma, or a disability.

Why Employees Resist Change

It may be more important to understand why employees resist change than to know why they embrace it. The objective is to anticipate why the employees may resist the change and address it up front. This is an area in which most companies would receive low marks. However, dealing effectively with undesirable changes is critical. Here, honesty and communication are key. Share the decision-making rationale with the employees. If there's a good level of trust between employees and management, and if management is very likeable, much of the resistance can be overcome.

Employees may resist change for the following reasons:

- They don't understand the change. It's not properly communicated.
- They don't feel a need to change. They don't see its importance.
- They conclude the change won't have the desired result or may even worsen their circumstances. They don't believe.
- They don't know how to make the desired change.
- They think the change requires too much additional energy and effort.
- They fear the ramifications if they are unable to achieve the desired change. They feel insecure.
- They have a general inherent aversion to change. They are fearful or uncomfortable.
- They perceive that the change will not be reinforced or rewarded.
- They see the same old thing.

Stay Focused on the Trend, Not the Backslide

As we've mentioned, change is difficult for people. If it weren't we would all be those things that our supervisor, spouse, children, and religious leaders want us to be. When an employee has taken ownership of an issue and is making improvements, it's vital that managers appreciate the pattern of human change, as depicted in Figure 11.2.

Employees don't change in a straight line. As illustrated in Figure 11.2, employees experience three different periods when attempting to improve. These are periods of improvement, stagnation, and regression. It's impor-tant to realize everyone is going to experience regression periods—when it seems all gains have been lost. If we look for the negative in others, we'll be quick to point out, "See, I told you that so and so wouldn't change." However, if we're looking for the good in people, and have seen strong improvement periods, we'll realize that relapses are natural events in the pattern of human change. Managers must stay focused on the trend of the improvement, not on the regression periods.

Make sure you're periodically complimentary during your employees' improvement periods (but don't overdo it). This is important because

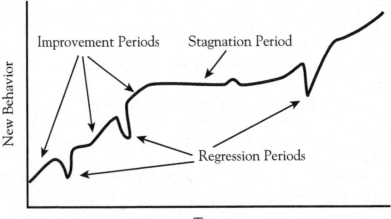

As employees change:
- Look for the trend, not the regressions
- Be complimentary during improvement periods
- Assume positive intentions

FIGURE 11.2: The *Pattern of Human Change*

intervening only when employees relapse may discourage them from continuing to complete their development plan. Make sure that you're giving employees only a few issues to work out at one time.

People Revert to Their Original Style under Stress

One of the major reasons people fall into regression periods is that they encounter a perceived stress. An example of this would be when a boxer who fights as a brawler decides he'll become a boxer for an upcoming fight. The first time he gets hit hard, he automatically reverts back to his street-fighting, hard-punching style. This is also true for any employee who has made considerable improvement. Managers should coach their employees before highly stressful events, making sure they self-monitor to avoid regression.

Some Helpful Techniques

If you're attempting to modify your employees' or managers' style of interacting with others, a useful method is to separate their intent from their style. This will allow them to work on their style issue without becoming overly defensive. They won't interpret their conversation with you as if you're telling them they're not good people. For example, begin the discussion by saying, "I know you have a good heart and your intentions are good. However, your interpersonal or management style suggests to others that your intent is not honorable. I know this is not the case, so let's take some time to examine how others are perceiving you as a result of your current style."

Another technique for reducing an employee's initial defense mechanisms is to couch the issue in the context of perception versus reality. You may say, "I know in reality that you're working hard on this project; however, the perception is that you're not. And the terrible thing is that, unfortunately, perception is reality. Someone's perception of you could lead to your termination—that's reality. So you need to start acting in a fashion that changes others' perception of you."

Sometimes Termination Is the Best Answer

All Human Resources professionals know that the two things managers dislike the most are writing performance appraisals and terminating employees. A concerted effort should be undertaken to coach employees through their issue. However, if significant progress hasn't occurred, and if a certain employee is not suitable for another position within the organization, termination is appropriate. Countless managers don't want to go through the emotions associated with firing someone. The result of this apprehension is to reduce operational output, teamwork, and perhaps quality. World-class companies require world-class employees—accept nothing less.

Just as a sideline, the worst thing you can do is to hire a replacement worse than the person fired. In this situation you lose credibility. You may hear the employees say, "This guy is even worse than the one they just fired. So why did they fire him?" Therefore, make sure your replacement is a stronger performer.

We have dedicated an entire chapter to the human change process because continuous improvement requires change. In addition, continuous improvement is essential if a company wants to survive and thrive in this globally competitive marketplace. At Microchip, we use the following phrase: "In times of change, the learners inherit the earth. And the learned are beautifully equipped to deal with a world that no longer exists."

This is one of the most profound statements that we have come across in our years of managing change and continuous improvement. This is because employees are usually comfortable with the status quo. A change exposes them to risks and uncertainties. It requires employees to change their methods and behaviors. We use the aforementioned statement to stress that the world is constantly changing and moving ahead. If employees don't change fast enough, they'll be left with skills that are no longer applicable in the new world.

12

The Transformation of Charlie Campbell

THE PREVIOUS CHAPTER outlined a methodology that managers could utilize to improve their employees' ability to adapt and perform. This chapter shows you the method in action. In an attempt to make the process more real, we have composed an interesting in-depth case study. You'll witness the struggles Charlie Campbell creates for himself by not taking ownership of the things he needs to improve. You'll see the life-changing impact one manager has on Charlie and the power of unleashing Charlie's true potential.

The human change process was illustrated earlier, in Figure 11.1. The objective of this process is for managers to get employees to take ownership of their problems in order to improve themselves. Unfortunately, employees often fall short of this objective. They may refuse to accept the validity of the issue, or they may unfairly place the blame on others. Employees may say they've changed, but they may just be playing a game with you. They can take ownership of the issue but might be unwilling to or incapable of making the needed improvement. Charlie's experiences led him through each of these stages.

Charlie's Background

Charlie Campbell was born in the early fall of 1978. He was the only child of Cliff and Lenore Campbell. Cliff was a tall, heavyset man with huge hands. His thick fingers were the result of years spent lifting machinery and tightening bolts. Cliff was a man of few words, becoming gregarious only with the inducement of bourbon. His copious consumption of bourbon was a Friday and Saturday night ritual. Colleagues and friends considered Cliff's quietness a natural personality trait. Charlie's interpretation was that his father had no interest in him. This father and son relationship was marked by an absence of dialogue and affection.

Cliff was a mechanic for the Sherman Tool and Die Company. He joined Sherman's on his return from a three-year stint in the army. He started out as the parts runner, retrieving parts from various warehouses throughout Detroit. Cliff considered the position beneath his qualifications, but he needed a job and it was an entry point into the civilian workforce. By year's end, Cliff's strong work ethic was recognized with a promotion to apprentice mechanic. Cliff found contentment as a mechanic. He liked the routine and independence it brought. Cliff labored in this position without further career aspirations for the next twenty-six years.

The Campbell family resided in a small house on 34th Street in a quaint Detroit neighborhood built in the 1950s. The large front porches wrapped around the sides of the homes as if to suggest they played a noteworthy role in daily life. The narrow front yards were lined with mature maple trees. In the summer, the trees' canopy provided shade for endless games of stickball. The boys played stickball until calls for dinner were shouted from the porches or open windows.

Detroit's frigid winters were fueled by steady northern winds that became vicious as they blew across Lake Michigan. The shortened days and extended nights that accompanied winter seemed to depress Charlie. He spent the winters hunched over his computer or watching television in the family room. This routine was interrupted by the occasional visit from one of Charlie's two childhood friends. Charlie's dampened spirits lifted only with the appearance of spring. The winter thaw allowed Charlie to once again freely roam the neighborhood and resume the stickball contests.

In 1992, Charlie entered Detroit's Midtown High School. Midtown High was a typical high school nestled at the southwestern edge of the city. It served mostly middle-class kids from the surrounding suburbs. Midtown was known for having a dominating football program, with four state championships in a nine-year stretch.

Charlie was handsome by most standards. He wasn't homecoming king material, but he remained the focus of many girls' conversations. His tall, slender physique and attractive face set him apart from the other boys. Charlie's avoidance of change kept him in the same attire he'd worn in junior high. His regular attire consisted of blue jeans, white tee shirt, and dark socks, finished off with a thick black belt.

Charlie maintained a 3.0 grade point average, excelling in hands-on-oriented courses. His best subjects were auto shop, industrial engineering, and computers. Like his father, Charlie was good with his hands. So, auto shop came easily but failed to stimulate his intellect. That's probably why he enjoyed computers. They were hands-on, highly structured, and intriguing, and they required minimal human interaction.

These four characteristics of computers were congruent with Charlie's dominant personality traits. From a young age, Charlie was drawn to highly structured activities, marked by repetition and predictability. He liked to feel in control, and was considered by most to be rigid. Charlie was, however, a curious person who readily learned new subjects compatible with his interests. Alternatively, if the subject failed to intrigue him, Charlie performed poorly.

By high school, it was apparent that Charlie had also inherited his father's quietness, aloofness, and resistance to change. He seemed uneasy when interacting with others. Charlie quickly drew conclusions about a person's shortcomings. He was always on the lookout for people's flaws, and it showed in his dialogue and posture. Needless to say, Charlie was not a people person.

The only people Charlie conversed with in any real sense were Robert Hastings and Bo Carson, his best friends since grade school. His negative demeanor toward others impeded new friendships. But that was okay with Charlie; no additional friendships were required. This soon changed when he was introduced to Sharon Bidwell, two months into their senior year.

Meeting girls was not Charlie's forte. He always felt awkward around women. Charlie did not have an effective opening line, and if he stumbled into one, he wouldn't know how to perpetuate the conversation. After being introduced to Sharon, his need for a captivating opening line ceased. Sharon made the initial gesture. "You know, Charlie, I've seen you around," she commented with a voice couched in flirtation. "I'm going to the cafeteria. Would you like to come?" she inquired. This walk to the cafeteria would change the course of Charlie's life. Charlie and Sharon would wed two years later.

Charlie's Problems Begin

In 1998, Charlie graduated from Val Vista Community College with an AA degree in Computer Science. He accepted a job at Up & Running, a computer repair shop on Woodward Avenue in downtown Detroit. Dan Randall, who had opened the shop eight years earlier, owned it outright. He had begun the venture with 3 employees, and now the thriving business had 27 employees.

Charlie was hired as a computer technician. His primary duties were to diagnose and repair PCs. Charlie was the newest technician on the staff, so occasionally he was required to fill in at the front counter. Charlie had been with the company for nine months and was considered an outstanding technician in terms of repairing computers. But Charlie would come to realize that just repairing computers in isolation was not enough.

Charlie hated working the counter. His heart and strengths lay in the repair shop, troubleshooting PCs, not up front dealing with the customers. The customers had too many questions for Charlie: "What do you think the problem is? I need it back right away. When can I pick it up? Can't you do better than that? How much will it cost? Do you think if I installed the new operating system, it'd solve the problem?"

Worst of all, Charlie resented that the customers knew nothing about computers. Charlie's favorite saying was, "It's an operator problem," implying that the vast majority of the repairs were caused by the customers' naiveté, not the hardware. When Dan Randall overheard Charlie's intolerance for the customers' lack of PC expertise, he'd say, "Charlie, we don't expect the customers to be experts on PCs; if they were, we'd be out of business." Charlie always piped down for a couple of days after that. Charlie's lack of interpersonal skills, negativity, and abruptness left customers with an unfavorable impression of the shop. This didn't bother Charlie because his real job was to fix computers.

Charlie thought that everything was going great. He didn't realize that several other repair technicians didn't like working with him. Charlie's negativity, aloofness, and lack of common courtesy rubbed them the wrong way. When asking for another technician's assistance, he was too blunt and unappreciative. He'd say, "Hey, Bob. Come here right now and hold this." There was an absence of common politeness because he didn't say such things as, "Please, if you have a minute, could you help me for a second?" Adding insult to injury, Charlie never bothered to say, "Thank you" or "I appreciate your help."

Charlie Lacks Awareness

After receiving complaints about Charlie from customers and coworkers, Dan Randall discussed the situation with Charlie. They met in Mr. Randall's office on Friday afternoon. Mr. Randall initiated the conversation. As usual, Mr. Randall came right to the point. "Charlie, frankly, I'm not satisfied with your work. I've received complaints about you from customers and the other technicians."

Charlie looked up with disbelief. "I'm one of the best techs in the shop. I don't like working the counter, but no customer has ever complained to me about my service," he said in a defensive and assertive voice. "I think that we all give good customer service around here. Come on, Dan. The other techs are all kind of weird, you know that. I don't know where this is coming from."

Mr. Randall was taken aback by Charlie's comments. He thought, "If Charlie feels so strongly about this, maybe I'm overreacting to the feedback. The techs are kind of a weird bunch and the customers can be overly demanding." After a pause, Mr. Randall said, "Okay, Charlie. Let's just try to do better and work as a team."

Charlie stood and replied, "No problem." He then headed back to the repair shop. As he made his way down the hall, Charlie was thinking, "This is all so stupid."

Goal of This Stage: *The manager coaches the employee to gain an awareness of the issue.*

What Transpired: *The problem with Charlie was real. However, Charlie's strong denial of its existence prompted doubt in the mind of Mr. Randall. Therefore, Mr. Randall lost his conviction.*

The Outcome: *Since Charlie didn't believe there was a problem, and Mr. Randall has let it go, no improvement was realized. In fact, Charlie might have harbored negative feelings toward the customers and coworkers for complaining to his boss. The way this conversation was left, the situation was likely to get worse.*

How the Manager Could Have Been More Effective: *Mr. Randall should have done his homework prior to the meeting. He should have gathered specific examples of Charlie's undesirable behavior. He should have anticipated Charlie's reaction and formulated a strategy to effectively combat his response. Mr. Randall should have kept pressing the issue and not accepted Charlie's dismissal of the problem. The meeting was too short to achieve the objective; the situation required more time.*

Charlie Blames Others

Mr. Randall may have let Charlie off the hook, but he was keeping a close eye on him. Charlie went on as if the meeting had never happened. At least it appeared that way on the surface. The more Charlie ruminated on the comments made by the customers and his coworkers, the angrier he became. In subtle ways his shortcomings became more prevalent. His rough edges became even rougher. His negativity appeared more often.

Meanwhile, Mr. Randall had become resentful of Charlie. After the meeting he realized that he'd let Charlie off the hook. Even worse, Charlie's behavior was not improving. He was still receiving periodic complaints about Charlie. "Clearly he did not get the message," Mr. Randall concluded. Mr. Randall decided that he'd have one more meeting with Charlie to resolve the issue once and for all. He thought, "Charlie is an outstanding technician and will be difficult to replace, but enough is enough."

Mr. Randall sent his secretary, Barbara Taylor, to find Charlie and bring him to the office. On the way to the office Charlie made small talk with Barbara. But he was really thinking, "Here we go again. I hate this stuff." As Charlie's eyes found Mr. Randall's face, he knew he was in deep trouble.

"Charlie, sit down," Mr. Randall said. "Charlie, I'm not happy with the results of our previous meeting."

Charlie cut in, "I thought we agreed that there wasn't a problem after all."

Mr. Randall replied, "No, Charlie, you concluded there was no problem, not me. I'm sorry, but things must change. I built this business from scratch. And I built it on customer service, quality work, and teamwork. Eight years of hard work, long days, and no real personal life. Those are my values and that is my commitment. What is yours?"

Charlie replied, "I know you've worked hard, Dan."

Mr. Randall said, "Customer service and teamwork are vital to this business' success. This time let me give you a few specific examples of where you fell short. Last week you yelled at Ed to get over and help you. Ed is a senior tech and he's not responsible for helping you. If you wanted his assistance you should have asked nicely. On Wednesday I saw you tell a customer to fill out her own paperwork. You know we complete all paperwork for the customers. We don't want to create more hassles for them. We want to reduce their hassles. Charlie, you're one of my best technicians. How can you eliminate these issues?"

Charlie answered, "OK, Dan, I think your criticism is justified. I've never been good with people. This is not the first time I've heard these types of complaints. So we're in agreement that I have a problem, an area I need to improve. But what you're not seeing, Dan, is that it's not my fault. I'm not trying to blame others, but if I want help around here I have to shout at people. I've tried asking nicely, and the other techs say they're too busy. If you were me, you'd be blunt with them, too. And as far as the customers go, you know they create most of their own problems and can be a pain in the side. If you wouldn't assign me to the front desk, when I really belong in the repair shop, there wouldn't be a problem. I can't keep going back and forth without getting frustrated. Nobody could."

"Charlie, we've never experienced an issue like this with the other technicians we've asked to work the front counter," commented Mr. Randall.

"But I'm sure they didn't work as hard as I do," was Charlie's response.

Silence filled the office as Mr. Randall paused to consider his course of action. "Charlie, I don't want to play the blame game with you. You can blame the customers or your coworkers, but you continue to be at the center of these issues. I've decided to let you go."

"You're firing me?" Charlie responded in disbelief.

"Yes, I'm letting you go. I will give you two weeks' pay as severance."

Charlie's expression turned from anger to fear. "Mr. Randall, I have a wife to support and a mortgage to pay. How am I going to tell my wife?"

Mr. Randall concluded the conversation by saying, "I'm sorry, Charlie. My decision is final."

Goal of This Stage: *The manager moves the employee beyond just blaming the environmental factors that are contributing to the issues.*

What Transpired: *Mr. Randall achieved some progress in describing the issues with Charlie. Charlie accepted the existence of the issues, but blamed his situation on everyone else.*

The Outcome: *Charlie acknowledged his weaknesses and the need to improve someday. However, he took no ownership for the issue and made no commitment to change. He felt that his unacceptable behavior and performance were the fault of the environment.*

How the Manager Could Have Been More Effective: *If Charlie hadn't been such a valuable employee, Mr. Randall's approach would have been appropriate. For a small business, termination would have been the best course of action. Mr. Randall did an excellent job stressing why it was critical for Charlie to address the problem. He stayed on course and maintained his conviction. Mr. Randall also got Charlie to acknowledge the issues by giving specific examples. We knew Charlie got it when he said, "I've never been good with people and I have heard this kind of thing before." Given that Charlie was one of Mr. Randall's best technicians and that Mr. Randall will incur the lost time and expense* associated with hiring and training a new individual, he should have done more to coach Charlie through the problem.

Mr. Randall could have spent more time helping Charlie see how he was contributing to the problem. With further discussions and direct coaching, there is a good chance Charlie could have made enough progress to resolve the problem. Moreover, Mr. Randall needed to get Charlie to realize the many benefits associated with making a sincere attempt to improve this situation. These benefits include keeping his job, greater promotional potential, increased career opportunities, and enhanced personal relations outside of work.

Charlie Plays the Game

After losing his job at Up & Running, Charlie went through a difficult period. It took him five months to land a new job. He ran through his savings. Even worse, he had to ask his father for a loan. As Charlie anticipated, paying the interest on the loan involved tolerating his father's ridicule. Cliff's favorite shaming lines included, "Charlie, have you got my money yet? I never had to borrow money from my dad."

Charlie's marriage was in a shambles. He and Sharon were constantly arguing over money. Charlie would yell at Sharon for buying what he considered nonessential items at the grocery store. Each time the credit card bill arrived, a fight was sure to follow. "Sharon, what is this expense for? Why did you buy something at that place?" Charlie would say in disbelief.

Charlie was spending much of the day at home. This placed added strain on the marriage. Sharon and Charlie got to know each other better than they wanted. Sharon was used to roaming the home freely. Now, as she went by the family room, there was Charlie, on the couch, drinking beer and criticizing the world. "Sharon, come here and see this guy on the TV. He's a total idiot," Charlie would insist. "Sharon, grab me a beer while you're in the kitchen," he'd demand. This all became too much for her. After a huge argument Sharon moved to her sister's home in Boston.

Charlie finally landed a job at a national electronics store in downtown Detroit. He was hired as the supervisor of the computer department. The store manager, Dean McCarthy, gave Charlie the position despite his concerns over Charlie's people skills. The store was under intense criticism concerning the sales associates' lack of computer expertise. Many of the customers knew more about computers than the sales associates who were assisting them. The corporate people concluded this lack of expertise was the source of the store's declining revenue. Computer sales had fallen consecutively for six months, while competitor revenue had increased. The store was clearly losing market share.

Dean had better candidates on file than Charlie, but they lacked adequate computer knowledge. So Dean compromised his selection criteria and chose Charlie. Dean knew he could be betting his job on Charlie's ability to raise the staff's technical expertise. If sales continued to fall, Dean would have no place to hide. Charlie didn't know it, but Dean needed Charlie as much as Charlie needed the job.

Charlie woke one Tuesday morning at 6:05 A.M. to the blaring sound of his bedside alarm clock. As always, he postponed that first step into the new day by hitting the snooze button. Charlie didn't cherish much in life, but these extra five minutes of rest were at the top of the list. Charlie loathed waking so early just so he could fight the morning commute. But the store was located in downtown Detroit, and that was forty-five minutes from the house. The regional manager was coming by the store to meet with Dean and the store supervisors at 8:00 A.M.

Most of all, Charlie hated waking up alone. Sharon had called the previous night and asked for a divorce. Even though they were separated, Charlie was shocked by the news. Everyone familiar with the couple knew that the divorce was inevitable. Everyone, that is, but Charlie. He never even truly saw it coming. Maybe that's what hurt the most. But awareness and sensitivity weren't Charlie's strong points.

Meanwhile, Dean was driving into the store. It was now apparent to him that Charlie's people skills were inadequate for his supervisory position. Charlie was recreating the same kind of issues that got him fired from Up & Running. Dean was angry with himself for selecting Charlie. He thought, "I knew I shouldn't have hired him. But he was the only one with adequate computer expertise." He concluded, "Everyone hates working with Charlie. But if I fire him, the corporate people will think I'm incapable of turning around the floundering sales. I have to make Charlie successful somehow."

The next day Dean met with Charlie to discuss the issues surrounding Charlie's negative attitude as well as his lack of interpersonal, customer service, teamwork, and people management skills. The meeting was relatively short. As usual, Charlie began blaming the environmental factors. "The customers are flakes, the coworkers are weird, and the employees know nothing about computers," he told Dean.

Dean was nice, but firm, saying, "Charlie, improvement in these areas isn't optional. If you want the job you'll have to develop your people skills."

Charlie went back to the sales floor. He was thinking, "I hate this job! I'm so sick of dealing with people. I need a job where I can just work on computers and not have to deal with people. But man, I really need this job. I'm just going to have to play the game and not get in any more trouble." This time Charlie was running scared. He would play the game and be nice to everyone.

Goal of This Stage: *If the manager concludes he needs the employee, but the employee won't take any meaningful ownership for how he's contributing to the issues, the manager must manage the employee at the behavioral level. At a minimum the manager should make the employee act accordingly.*

What Transpired: *Dean McCarthy laid down the law at the behavioral level. He made his general expectations clear: "Be nice to people."*

The Outcome: *Charlie became fearful, which motivated him to attempt to behave differently while at the store. But Charlie failed to take any ownership for his contributions to the situation. Instead, he started playing the game of being nice to others and maintaining a positive disposition. Dean McCarthy will have to keep the pressure on Charlie to maintain the desired outcome.*

How the Manager Could Have Been More Effective: *Dean McCarthy spoke to Charlie in generalities. He didn't discuss specific examples in which Charlie's actions fell short of expectations. Dean didn't attempt to get Charlie to take ownership for the issues. Therefore, no developmental action plan was generated for Charlie. For someone who needs Charlie to succeed, Dean made little effort. This approach may cost Dean his job if he doesn't change strategies.*

Charlie Takes Ownership and Improves

It wasn't easy, but Charlie played the game. He had his bad days. However, in general, he followed the program. In fact, the more often Charlie was nice to customers and went the extra mile to service them, the easier it became. Yet he still needed to enhance his supervisory skills. He had developed as a manager, but further improvement was still warranted.

In March, Charlie received his first formal performance appraisal. Charlie had been with the company for one year. He had come to really like his job. Dean and Charlie met in Dean's office after lunch to review his performance. Dean told Charlie that overall it was a good first year. They both joked about the store's increased sales growth.

Dean commented, "Charlie, if we hadn't met our sales goals someone else would be giving you this performance appraisal." Charlie replied, "I doubt that. I'd have been sacrificed before they dealt with you."

They both laughed.

Dean said, "Charlie, you've come a long way since last March. You've made steady progress. I've gone over your accomplishments and strengths; now I'd like to focus on some developmental areas."

"Sure," Charlie said. He had come to respect and like Dean as a supervisor.

Dean continued, "I know that to some degree you're just playing the game. I guess that's what bothers me the most."

"I don't know what you mean."

"If you strengthened your managerial skills, you could manage your own store some day." Dean answered.

Charlie replied, "Oh, I'm not sure about that."

"No, Charlie, I'm not kidding. You trust my judgment, don't you?"

"You know I do," Charlie replied. "I don't have the background to be a great manager. My father couldn't manage his way out of a paper bag. None of my friends are managers and I studied computers in college, not business management."

"Charlie, to a large degree it's not your background that'll make you successful. It's your desire and commitment that truly count," assured Dean. "I manage an electronics store employing 33 people, with annual sales of $11 million. I don't have a business management degree. I've got a Master's in political science. You're as smart as I am. You just haven't been as hungry. You haven't been willing to own up to your weaknesses and overcome them. That's where I have you beat. We don't overcome our weaknesses and learn new skills overnight. It takes real commitment, lots of hard work, time, and a little luck," Dean said in earnest. "Charlie, let's discuss your career goals. Would you like to be the store manager some day?"

"Yes, I would," Charlie said with a newly found confidence and enthusiasm. "I don't want to just run the computer department the rest of my life."

Dean said, "Charlie, there are two main things you need to work on if you're going to be the store manager. First, your employees think you don't take enough time training them. Second, they don't like the way you manage people."

Charlie looked down and then said, "Dean, I'm extremely busy, but I spend plenty of time training my people. I don't agree with their assessment. And as far as my people skills go, I'm really not that bad anymore. I don't know what they want from me!"

"Charlie, let's stop right here. You just said you wanted to become store manager and you would dedicate yourself to improving. But I don't think you truly meant it," Dean said in a serious tone.

"Of course I meant it," Charlie insisted.

Dean replied, "It's not easy to face your weaknesses head on and develop new skills. Well, Charlie, let me ask you a question. If I wanted to measure your effectiveness, anyone's effectiveness, as a manager, who would I ask?"

Charlie thought for a moment and then said, "A person's boss, the people who work for him, coworkers, and customers, I guess."

"That's right Charlie. So why are you so quick to dismiss your employees' assessments and feedback? Let me take a guess. Is it because you see them as a burden, rather than taking pride in them? Is it because you measure managerial success in terms of sales and output? Managerial success should be viewed as an internally driven motivation to be an outstanding, well-rounded manager; even when no one's watching."

Dean then explained, "Charlie, I see you're stuck in the blaming game.

You're disguising your sincerity about becoming an excellent manager. You say you want to be the store manager, while dismissing the feedback of the interested parties."

Charlie sat quietly. Dean broke the silence, "Talk to me, Charlie. These are important issues regarding your future success here or wherever you end up."

Dean continued, "Let's say that you're mostly right about your criticism of your employees' misconceptions of you as a manager. So, for now we'll say you're correct and we'll put their contributions to the issue aside. In what way have you contributed to their negative perception of you? Are you willing to examine that?"

Charlie replied, "You want me to take ownership for my contribution to the situation. That's fair enough. But I'm not sure that I'm comfortable discussing that."

"Why not, Charlie?" Dean asked.

"Well, you may hold what I say against me. It's easier and safer to just blame others for their contributions to the issue," Charlie responded.

Dean said, "This is what I mean about disguising your genuine sincerity to improve. If you were truly motivated to become an outstanding manager and really did trust me, you'd seek out this information on your own. You'd be hungry for the inputs and feedback. It's those who don't want to improve who don't want the feedback. Do you think that's right, Charlie?"

"Yes, I think that's correct."

"Charlie, this is your crossroad. One path leads you in a circle and the other to greater heights. Only you can choose. It's a matter of what you want out of life. You can choose to let your weaknesses slow your progress or you can embrace change and continuous improvement. Both paths extract a price. So, what will it be, Charlie?"

Dean continued, "Charlie, over the next week or so, I'd like you to think about where these attitudes and behaviors come from. Begin monitoring yourself to ensure your background doesn't continue to govern your attitudes and behaviors, that it doesn't impede your progress. Try to figure out why you don't seem to value other people and why you actively look for the negatives in each situation. I suggest this because these underlying values and personality traits are inhibiting your progress. See, our underlying personality traits and values fuel our actions and attitudes. If you can begin to consciously manage your values and traits, rather than letting them manage you, you'll gain control over your attitudes and actions."

Charlie said, "Wow, you made some good points. You've given me a lot to think about. I appreciate the interest you've taken in my development and career. So, let me address your earlier question. How am I contributing to my employees' unfavorable perception of me? Well, I need to take some ownership here. It's true that I don't train my people enough and that I'm not a great people manager. I could've spent more time personally training the guys. I'm busy, but in this job I'll always be too busy to develop my employees if I don't establish dedicated training sessions. Today I use the most experienced sales associate on the shift to train the new guys. But if that person is not a good trainer, or doesn't know much, I can see where the problem lies. Maybe I can talk to the guys individually over the next few days and get their input."

"Great start," Dean said.

Charlie suggested, "I could assign one person to be a designated trainer. If I'm not available to train the new sales associate, the trainer could take over. I also could develop some short training classes—a class on printers, one on monitors, and so forth."

Dean gently interrupted, "Charlie, don't go too fast, or you'll lose the opportunity to show your staff your new management style. You'll also miss their valuable input and feedback. Improvement is a team sport. You've got a great team. Involve them in the improvement efforts. If you develop all the solutions to the current training issue, you'll lose the opportunity to involve your staff. You'll get greater buy-in and commitment from your employees if they help draft the solutions."

Dean continued, "In addition, if an employee doesn't follow the plan that the team agreed upon, it'll be easier to hold that person accountable. You can say, 'We all agreed, including you, that training should be done this way. But now you're not living up to your commitment.' Then the employee becomes the bad guy or problem, not you. This means you reprimand such employees because they did not meet their commitment to you or the group. This will help to reduce the perception that you're just an overly demanding manager. Remember, Charlie, fostering employee involvement and development increases employees' commitment and job satisfaction. It also enhances their respect for, and how much they like, the manager."

Then Dean suggested, "Charlie, now that you've taken ownership to improve the situation, we should write you a development plan. Together, let's establish a development plan that can help guide you in making the needed improvements."

Charlie replied, "Great, that'll be helpful."

It was getting late, so Dean said, "We'll work on this next week. Until then, if you have any thoughts concerning the development plan, jot them down."

Dean and Charlie met the following week and documented Charlie's personalized development plan. Following is the plan.

Charlie Campbell's Development Plan

Career Aspirations:
- Short-term: To be recognized as the most effective department supervisor
- Long-term: To be promoted to the position of store manager

Goals:
- Strengthen managerial skills, with an emphasis on people skills
- Enhance interpersonal skills
- Maintain the best-trained department in the store
- Be recognized as a team player (short-term) and a team leader (long-term)

Actions and Timeline:
- Continuously monitor self to ensure that attitude and behavior are consistent with the stated goals
- Next quarter, attend two courses on managing people
- Conduct an anonymous survey of the employees to get feedback on

management style and areas in which the operation can improve; incorporate feedback into this development plan

- Hold short monthly meetings with each employee in the computer department
- Actively look for opportunities to involve employees in decision-making and improvement activities
- With the participation of the employees, construct an employee-training program
- Participate in the Storewide Continuous Improvement Operational Team
- Meet with Dean McCarthy for feedback and coaching once per quarter
- Take three business classes at a local college in the next year to increase knowledge of the purely business aspects of managing the store

What to Avoid:
- Statements that are perceived as putdowns by employees like can't you do that, get to it, you should know that, anyone else would be done by now—(emphasize better phrasing)
- References to how much you know and how little the other person knows
- General reactions and statements that give people the perception that you're highly critical and negative
- Competitive tendencies with the other department supervisors

Goal of This Stage: *The manager helps the employee take ownership of how the employee is contributing to the issue and works with the employee on establishing a developmental plan. The developmental plan must be realistic.*

What Transpired: *Dean McCarthy demonstrated the impact an excellent manager can have on an employee's success. His ability to manage Charlie at a deeper level than just the behavioral level was impressive.*

The Outcome: *Dean was able to get Charlie to take full responsibility for his contributions toward the undesirable situation. He got Charlie motivated to im-*

prove himself. Finally, he constructed a documented development plan to guide Charlie's development.

How the Manager Could Have Been More Effective: No recommendations. It'll be important for Dean to stay on top of the situation and continue to coach Charlie.

Update on Charlie Campbell

It took a great deal of hard work, but Charlie successfully completed his development plan. Moreover, he received an outstanding rating on his next annual performance appraisal. The subsequent year, Dean McCarthy moved to Phoenix to run the company's newest store. Thirteen months later, Charlie was promoted to store manager. Following in Dean's footsteps, Charlie is now known for his excellent managerial skills.

The improvements Charlie made in the workplace spilled over to his personal life. His enhanced interpersonal skills and generally positive disposition have impressed everyone but his father. Some things never change. Charlie met and married Lisa Gilbert last August.

Dean and Charlie talk on occasion. Last month Dean was in Detroit so he stopped by the store to say hello. As he entered the store, he saw Charlie directing employees and answering customers' inquiries. He stopped at the CD shelves for a moment, observing Charlie from a distance. He reflected on the path, the fork in the road, that Charlie chose to pursue two years earlier—the improvement path that brought him to where he is today. Now Charlie had a great job and a marvelous wife, and was a happier person. Dean realized the impact a manager can have on an employee's life.

Dean made his way over to Charlie. As he approached Charlie he took notice of his nametag, which read, Store Manager, *Charles* Campbell, not Charlie. Dean thought, "That says it all."

Section Four

Building the Aggregate System

13

Strategic Formula

THE STRATEGIC FORMULA consists of the company's vision, mission, strategies, business plans, and P&L/balance sheet models. Forming the strategic formula is the first and most critical step in building your *Aggregate System*. If your strategic formula is fundamentally flawed, the *Aggregate System* approach—or any other one—will be futile. The various elements that constitute the strategic formula must be realistic, on target, and achievable.

If your strategic formula is unsound, the *Aggregate System* may actually be detrimental to your business. The efficiencies gained by utilizing the system may hasten the company's failure. There is no benefit to aligning and integrating the entire enterprise to a faulty strategic formula. It spells trouble if you've set incorrect or unachievable strategies for fulfilling the company's mission. Therefore, the correct expertise and experience to build a sound strategic formula are paramount.

Ownership of the strategic formula lies with the CEO, who will ultimately be held accountable for the success of the formula. However, the components of the formula should be developed utilizing a team approach. The CEO selects the team members and leads the team. The CEO must ensure that people from all major departments are involved, especially individuals from finance, marketing, and sales who not only understand the market but also have street smarts. The team may include board members. In private companies, the owners would typically participate. On occasion the CEO may want to involve individuals not affiliated with the enterprise. This would include experts from academia or consultants. Be careful not to let the outsiders over-influence the process. The outside consultants may be experts in their piece of the Aggregate Business Puzzle (see Figure 2.2), but it is the CEO's job to control the process and keep an eye on the big picture. Finally, utilize appropriate research specific to the industry.

This chapter briefly outlines seven broad steps involved in constructing a strategic formula. This is a dynamic process with ample reiteration. Therefore, the steps are not necessarily sequential. The chapter focuses on the process of establishing the formula, not the actual content. Each firm's vision, mission, strategies, and business plans are unique. This book aims to teach you how to create a culture to ensure a strategic formula is realized, not how to establish a new company, formulate strategies to prosper in a given marketplace, or create business plans. As there are numerous books and articles on the latter subjects, the discussion of them will be limited.

Step One: Understand the Marketplace and Your Niche

Team members need a comprehensive grasp of the marketplace and the niche they'll occupy. They should analyze relevant market research, including trends and projections. They need to understand the predominant competitors' strengths, weaknesses, and recipes for success. The team must have a clear and compelling rationale of why they'll succeed. Do they have a better mousetrap? Have they concluded they'll outperform the existing competitors? Or will they fill an underserved space in the market? Small business owners may simply be chasing their dream to be their own boss.

In order to have a high probability of success the enterprise needs to have one or more of the following attributes: (1) superior service that builds customer loyalty, (2) products that are highly appealing to the targeted customer base, (3) proprietary products (e.g., patented products and technologies or products where it's difficult for customers to change sources), (4) geographic dominance (being the only company in a given locale that's readily accessible to customers), (5) a prestigious brand name (quality), or (6) a low-cost structure that provides an advantage in pricing. If you don't have one of these characteristics to provide a competitive advantage, you can easily be displaced in the marketplace.

Step Two: Define the Company Vision

The team should document their ultimate vision of the company: why the company was formed, the dream of what the company could be, its impact on the customers or community, what it'll look like if it's truly successful. The vision should be expressed in a straightforward, lofty statement. Microchip's vision is: "To be the best imbedded control company ever." Some other examples include: "Our vision is to make healthcare more affordable and accessible," "We allow individuals the freedom to execute their own stock transactions," "We integrate business software into one enterprise-wide system," or "We improve people's lives through sound financial planning." The vision will become more specific once the firm establishes its mission statement.

Step Three: Define the Mission of the Company

The mission represents the purpose of the company. It may include being a leading supplier of a particular technology, product, or service in a given industry. It may be to provide excellence in quality, customer service, or convenience. The focus may be on financial strength or increasing shareholders' equity.

The team should formalize the company's mission. The mission must be realistic but bold. Keep it simple, understandable, and reflective of the firm's general attitude. The mission should be articulated using a mission statement. Figure 13.1 provides examples of mission statements. Over time, the mission can be modified in response to changing expectations or circumstances.

Microchip Technology:

Microchip Technology Incorporated is a leading supplier of field-programmable embedded control solutions by manufacturing the popular PICmicro® RISC microcontrollers which serve 8- and 16-bit embedded control applications; a broad spectrum of high-performance linear and mixed-signal, power management and thermal management devices; and related non-volatile memory products. In order to contribute to the on-going success of customers, shareholders and employees, our mission is to focus resources on high-value, high-quality products and to continuously improve all aspects of our business, providing a competitive return on investment.

Source: Microchip Technology

FedEx Mission Statement:

FedEx Corporation will produce superior financial returns for its share-owners by providing high value-added logistics, transportation, and related information services through focused operating companies. Customer requirements will be met in the highest quality manner appropriate to each market segment served. FedEx Corporation will strive to develop mutually rewarding relationships with its employees, partners, and suppliers. Safety will be the first consideration in all operations. Corporate activities will be conducted to the highest ethical and professional standards.

Source: FedEx's website as of 2004. © 1995–2004 Federal Express Corporation

Procter & Gamble (Purpose):

We will provide branded products and services of superior quality and value that improve the lives of the world's consumers. As a result, consumers will reward us with leadership sales, profit, and value creation, allowing our people, our shareholders, and the communities in which we live and work to prosper.

Source: P&G's website as of 2004. © 2003 P&G

FIGURE 13.1: Examples of Mission Statements

Step Four: Define the Strategies Necessary to Achieve the Mission

Business strategies that achieve the company's mission can be external or internal. External strategies represent the strategies that'll lead you to the desired position in the market. Internal strategies are the approaches you'll take to maximize your execution, reach your cost goals, and generally run the operation. The team should establish the company's overall external and internal strategies. At this stage, the team is forming the big picture, not bogging itself down in the details.

The external strategies specify such things as the products or services you'll offer, how you will position the products or services in the marketplace, and how they will be differentiated from those of competitors. The external strategies should show what your initial marketing campaigns will focus on, the general price points the market will bear, and the quality and cycle times expected by the customer. In addition, you need to answer these questions: Will the focus be on industry-standard products or proprietary products? What sales channels (retail, OEMs, or distributors) will be utilized? How will the firm gain stability through diversity in product portfolio, product applications, technologies, broad customer base, and geographical sales? You should determine the geographic locations of sales, customer service, and technical offices, as well as discuss what role the Internet will play.

The internal strategies identify how the team will approach the formation, capabilities, and standards of its internal systems. These are the systems utilized to bring the products and services to the marketplace. Will the product be designed and/or manufactured in house or by a vendor? What technology will be used? What are acceptable quality standards and cycle times for product development and manufacturing? The team should address each of these questions. The team may want to have a general discussion on what the Finance, Information Technology (IT), Legal, Planning, and Human Resources components of the enterprise should look like. In addition, the potential locations of the company's various facilities should be examined.

Step Five: Define the Core and Support Functions of Your Business

It's important for a company to define the core and support functions of its business. At Microchip the true objective is to produce "high-performance, low-cost products and services." This is the only thing the customer can be billed for. So it's imperative to understand the functions or operations within the business that directly produce, market, and sell the product or service.

When constructing your strategic formula, you should clarify the various functions or operations that constitute the enterprise. Break them into two categories: core functions and support functions. At Microchip, the core functions are the fundamental operations necessary to produce high-performance, low-cost products and services. In the end, the effectiveness of these functions is what the customer is willing to pay for. As illustrated in Figure 13.2, in a technology company such as Microchip, the core functions are Technology and Product Development, Manufacturing, and Marketing and Sales. Technology and Product Development create the products and services, Manufacturing produces them, and Marketing and Sales optimize their sale. By default, the support functions are all the remaining functions. In this case, support functions include Finance, Facilities, Human Resources, Information Technology (IT), Training, and Quality.

The categorization of core and support functions does not imply that employees in the support groups are not as critical as those in the core groups. Rather, it provides perspective on the operation, so you don't lose sight of the big picture. It defines the order of priority in which a CEO must ensure that the strategic formula is defined. Therefore, work to maximize the core functions and keep the support groups as lean as possible.

The core and support functions vary with different types of businesses. The core functions for a high-technology company will be different from those of a banking institution. In a technology company, technology is a core function, while in the banking industry, technology is a *support* function. Typically, core functions are limited to three to four functions. The rest are support functions. Figure 13.3 shows the categorization of core and support functions for a banking institution. Here, the core functions are

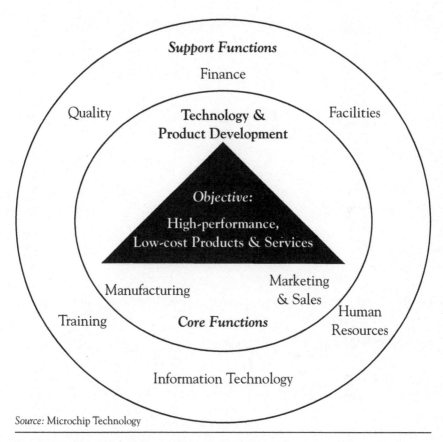

Figure 13.2: The Core and Support Functions of Microchip

Financial Product and Service Development, Branch Operations, and Administrative Services. Examples of support functions are Auditors, Facilities, Human Resources, Information Technology, Community Relations, and Software Support.

Step Six: Establish Your Business Plan

At this stage, the team converts the external and internal strategies into a definitive plan. The process starts by constructing a three- to five-year business plan. The plan should consist of the firm's annual goals and objectives

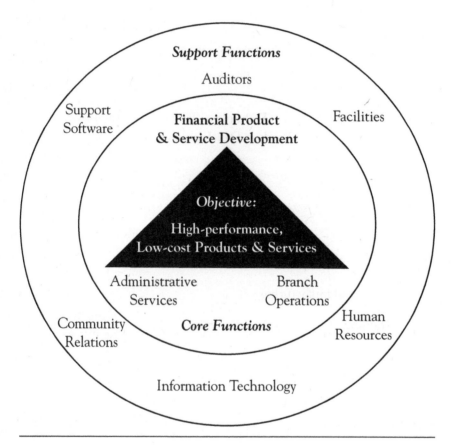

Figure 13.3: The Core and Support Functions of a Banking Institution

over the stated time frame. It should outline the product development activities, manufacturing efficiencies, and sales initiatives necessary to reach the revenue and profitability goals. It also includes a realistic projection of quarterly revenue growth, P&L, and the balance sheet.

The three- to five-year plan provides the framework for when the company constructs the annual operating plan (AOP). The AOP specifies the expected financial results based on quarterly sales and costs for the fiscal year. Here you detail the initiatives and expectations of the various functions within the enterprise that lead to achievement of the fiscal results.

Eventually, the AOP is broken down into quarterly objectives (e.g., management by objective [MBOs]) for each organization.

Step Seven: Determine the Organizational Structures, Boundaries, and Levels of Hierarchy

The team should discuss how they want to organize the company. They must identify how the key processes—such as research, product development, sales, and manufacturing—will be organized. The team needs to examine the optimum organizational structure and responsibilities to facilitate these processes. Avoid automatically adopting the traditional functional organizational structures. Too many levels of management can have an undesirable effect on continuous improvement and employee empowerment.

14

Selecting Your Core Values

THE PURPOSE OF the AGGREGATE SYSTEM is to systematically align and integrate every human aspect of the enterprise around a set of core values, producing a self-perpetuating, continuous-improvement culture designed for world-class excellence. This chapter will guide you through the methodology of establishing a team to specify your core values and the necessary rules to achieve them. You should complete this seven-step process over the course of several meetings.

In the preceding chapter you constructed your strategic formula. You stipulated your vision, mission, strategies, business plans, and P&L/balance sheet models for the enterprise—now the team must address the type of company culture that will provide the greatest probability of realizing the strategic formula. Assuming that you choose a values-based, highly empowered, continuous-improvement culture or a variation thereof, the process of selecting your customized culture begins with frank and heartfelt discussions. Be aware that these discussions can yield unrealistic conclusions on the potential cultural attributes. Keep the inputs flowing, but don't lose sight of their practicality and achievability. The quality of these meetings is critical since the culture will be designed based on their outcome.

Expect particular individuals to express strongly held opposing positions. People hold considerably different views on topics such as culture, values, rules, and characteristics of excellent managers and employees. These discussions will be dynamic, even confrontational at times. Therefore, establish ways in which participants can disagree without their egos or feelings getting damaged. For instance, gain consensus on the practice of agreeing to disagree, but with each individual accepting the group's decision and implementing it vigorously.

The team will be comprised of the CEO, senior executives, powerbrokers, and crucial employees. Although this is a group endeavor, the CEO must remain engaged in the sessions since he or she is obligated to role model the culture. Cultures that endure always require the CEO to role model them. Furthermore, the CEO must hold the staff accountable for practicing strategies, decisions, actions, and a management style consistent with the culture. With some executives this means coaching and for a few others it may mean termination.

A professional, unbiased facilitator should help the CEO lead these sessions. This will allow the participants to focus on the substance of the content rather than managing and recording the actual process of discovery. Have the group establish ground rules on process and conduct upfront. Restate and record the conclusions (your unique recipe for success) as the group proceeds through each of the seven steps.

Step One: Customize the Ten Key Elements of the *Aggregate System* to Define Your Desired Culture

The team should review Chapter 3, particularly Figure 3.1. Then customize these elements and their corresponding descriptions to match the team's management philosophy and strategic formula. This will provide the team with a general view of what the culture will look like. You're now actually building the culture.

Step Two: Determine the Aspects of the Business that Require Stated Public Values

Utilizing the elements of the *Aggregate System* and strategic formula, specify the company's core values. We have provided a limited list. Begin by expanding this list. Then assign the items in the list into classifications such as critical, important, and good. This ensures the focus is on the critical ones around which you're building the company culture. Be careful not to establish an excessive list.

Core Values

- Customers
- Quality
- Continuous improvement
- Employees
- Innovation
- Frugality and costs
- Financial strength (including revenue growth, profitability, etc.)
- Sharing company's prosperity
- Products and technologies
- Communication
- Teamwork
- Continuous learning
- Safety
- Cycle times
- Vendors, suppliers, and subcontractors
- Distributors and representatives
- Ethics and honesty
- Adaptability and flexibility
- Independence
- Competitiveness
- Assertiveness
- Recognition

Step Three: Construct Core Values Phrases

Step Three entails translating the values you've selected into descriptive phrases that employees can remember. For instance, Figure 14.1 shows Microchip's company values phrases. They state "Customers Are Our Focus," "Employees Are Our Greatest Strength," "Continuous Improvement Is Essential," and so forth. Procter & Gamble employs a slightly different format to express its core values, as illustrated in Figure 14.2. Finally, Figure 14.3 shows how General Electric chooses to document its values. Each company's approach to documenting its core values varies. There is no best format. The team should select the method that suits them. Remember, the crucial point is not that the values are documented, but rather that they are practiced.

Use phrases that are easy to remember and make a strong impact. For example, rather than stating, "Quality is important," you could say something more dramatic like "Quality is paramount" or "Quality will never be sacrificed." You may be wondering in what order you should place the core values. Should quality be listed first, or should the first item be customers or employees? There's no right answer—the team's preference will determine the answer. Employees will ask about this, so have your answer prepared.

The team must now turn to writing a text description that specifies what each core value phrase means. This is a considerable undertaking. It involves developing a detailed and clear description that employees can use to guide their actions. Moreover, it's the basis by which every system in the company will be designed to satisfy the value. Both the Procter & Gamble example in Figure 14.2 and the Microchip example in Figure 14.1 demonstrate excellent models for guiding the team through this process.

Step Four: Specify Essential Rules or Policies that Must Be Instilled in the Culture

Rules are an indispensable part of all societies and corporate cultures. In the business world, we primarily refer to rules as policies. They also take the form of procedures, manuals, operating guides, and specifications. Values-based company cultures embrace policies. However, they attempt to keep the rules to a minimum, striving to find that ideal balance between values and rules.

In Step Four, the team must determine in what areas rules will dominate the operation. The team must also decide in what situations they will want to avoid over-emphasizing rules. These are big picture conversations. Subgroups from each organization of the enterprise must define the appropriate policies and procedures for their function. There will be plenty of opportunity for each organization to make a detailed proposal at a later date. Listed here are a few examples of the areas to be discussed and recorded.

- Adherence to financial accounting standards
- Documentation of essential functions and enforcement
- Safety policies and procedures
- Adherence to and awareness of employment laws
- Disciplinary policies
- Environmental laws and compliance
- Wage and working conditions rules
- Vacations and sick policies
- Malfunctioning parts and returns policies

Step Five: Determine the General Approach to Motivate, Recognize, Reward, and Compensate Employees for Practicing the Core Values

The team should discuss and record their approaches for motivating, recognizing, rewarding, and compensating employees for practicing the core values. Further, the approaches they select should, by their very nature, work to retain employees and sustain job satisfaction. Make no mistake—company and individual employee performance should always be incorporated into the company's core values. If they're not, the strategic formula can never be attained.

The team must decide the approaches it will utilize (such as total compensation, variable compensation, merit-based practices, profit sharing, retirement schemes, and medical benefits) to align employees' practice of the core values in achievement of the strategic formula. Will you motivate employees by allowing them to directly share in the company's prosperity through stock options or restricted stock, Employee Stock Purchase Plan, and/or a quarterly cash bonus based on the company performance? If so, who should be eligible—just key employees or all employees, but at varying levels? These are the types of things to decide.

The team should also discuss how these approaches will be driven by the human systems as they are constructed. The actual method for achieving this is described in Chapter 17. At this stage, the team is required only to draw conclusions. Subgroups that have the functional responsibility and necessary expertise will construct the systems.

MICROCHIP

Customers Are Our Focus: We establish successful customer partnerships by exceeding customer expectations for products, services, and attitude. We start by listening to our customers, earning our credibility by producing quality products, delivering comprehensive services, and meeting commitments. We believe each employee must effectively serve their internal customers in order for Microchip's external customers to be properly served.

Quality Comes First: We will perform correctly the first time and maintain ISO 9001 and QS 9000 quality system certification to ensure customer satisfaction. We practice effective and standardized improvement methods, such as statistical process control, to anticipate problems and implement root cause solutions. We believe that when quality comes first, reduced costs follow.

Continuous Improvement Is Essential: We utilize the concept of "Vital Few" to establish our priorities. We concentrate our resources on continuously improving Vital Few while empowering each employee to make continuous improvements in their area of responsibility. We strive for constructive and honest self-criticism to identify improvement opportunities.

Employees Are Our Greatest Strength: We design jobs and provide opportunities promoting employee teamwork, productivity, creativity, pride in work, trust, integrity, fairness, involvement, development, and empowerment. We base recognition, advancement, and compensation on an employee's achievement of excellence in team and individual performance. We provide for employee health and welfare by offering competitive and comprehensive employee benefits.

FIGURE 14.1: Example of Company Values: Microchip

Products and Technology Are Our Foundation: We make ongoing investments and advancements in the design and development of our manufacturing process, device, circuit, system, and software technologies to provide timely, innovative, reliable, and cost effective products to support current and future market opportunities.

Total Cycle Times Are Optimized: We focus resources to optimize cycle times to our internal and external customers by empowering employees to achieve efficient cycle times in their area of responsibility. We believe that cycle time reduction is achieved by streamlining processes through the systematic removal of barriers to productivity.

Safety Is Never Compromised: We place our concern for safety of our employees and community at the forefront of our decisions, policies, and actions. Each employee is responsible for safety.

Profits and Growth Provide For Everything We Do: We strive to generate and maintain competitive rates of company profits and growth as they allow continued investment for the future, enhanced employee opportunity, and represent the overall success of Microchip.

Communication Is Vital: We encourage appropriate, honest, constructive, and ongoing communication in company, customer, and community relationships to resolve issues, exchange information, and share knowledge.

Suppliers and Distributors Are Our Partners: We strive to maintain professional and mutually beneficial partnerships with suppliers and distributors who are an integral link in the achievement of our mission and guiding values.

Professional Ethics Are Practiced: We manage our business and treat customers, employees, shareholders, investors, suppliers, distributors, community, and government in a manner that exemplifies our honesty, ethics, and integrity. We recognize our responsibility to the community and are proud to serve as an equal opportunity employer.

Source: Microchip Technology

FIGURE 14.1: Example of Company Values: Microchip (*continued*)

P&G is its people and the values by which we live.

We attract and recruit the finest people in the world. We build our organization from within, promoting and rewarding people without regard to any difference unrelated to performance. We act on the conviction that the men and women of Procter & Gamble will always be our most important asset.

Leadership
- We are all leaders in our area of responsibility, with a deep commitment to deliver leadership results.
- We have a clear vision of where we are going.
- We focus our resources to achieve leadership objectives and strategies.
- We develop the capability to deliver our strategies and eliminate organizational barriers.

Ownership
- We accept personal accountability to meet our business needs, improve our systems, and help others improve their effectiveness.
- We all act like owners, treating the Company's assets as our own and behaving with the Company's long-term success in mind.

Integrity
- We always try to do the right thing.
- We are honest and straightforward with each other.
- We operate within the letter and spirit of the law.
- We uphold the values and principles of P&G in every action and decision.
- We are data-based and intellectually honest in advocating proposals, including recognizing risks.

Passion for Winning
- We are determined to be the best at doing what matters most.
- We have a healthy dissatisfaction with the status quo.
- We have a compelling desire to improve and to win in the marketplace.

FIGURE 14.2: Example of Company Values: Procter & Gamble (P&G)

Trust

- We respect our P&G colleagues, customers, and consumers, and treat them as we want to be treated.
- We have confidence in each other's capabilities and intentions.
- We believe that people work best when there is a foundation of trust.

Source: P&G's website as of 2004. © 2003 P&G

FIGURE 14.2: Example of Company Values: Procter & Gamble (P&G) (*continued*)

MORE THAN JUST a set of words, these values embody the spirit of General Electric at its best. They reflect the energy and spirit of a company that has the solid foundation to lead change as business evolves. And they articulate a code of behavior that guides us through that change with integrity. The General Electric values are:

- **Passionate**
- **Curious**
- **Resourceful**
- **Accountable**
- **Teamwork**
- **Committed**
- **Open**
- **Energizing**

Source: GE's official company website as of February 2004. © 1997–2004 General Electric Company

FIGURE 14.3: Example of Company Values: General Electric

Step Six: Agree How Everyone Will Be Held Accountable for Practicing the Culture

This stage takes on two forms: (1) how do we measure if we're practicing our core values, and (2) what occurs if we're not? Measuring adherence to the core values begins with assessing whether you are coming closer to reaching the strategic formula. Moreover, assess compliance by utilizing anonymous annual employee surveys, focus groups, performance appraisals, one-on-one employee-manager meetings, luncheons with leaders and employees, and operational indicators.

If an organization, executive, manager, supervisor, or employee is consistently acting contrary to the core values there must be consequences. The action could take the form of systems improvement, setting clear expectations for compliance, training, counseling, disciplinary procedure, or termination. The CEO must be approachable so that he or she can accept feedback and make any warranted enhancements.

Step Seven: Communicate Core Values and Expected Characteristics of Managers and Employees

The team must develop a plan to communicate to the entire employee population the core values and expected characteristics of managers and employees. Communicate with executives, management, supervisors, and Human Resources first. Allow a little time for it all to settle in. Have them evaluate all aspects of their specific operation to ensure it aligns and integrates into the new culture and its core values.

Hold company-wide communication meetings where the CEO and executives describe the new culture, including the core values. Clarify the characteristics and performance expectations that all employees are expected to strive for. Inform employees that the core values will be used to construct the hiring criteria, job descriptions, performance appraisals, promotional criteria, Human Resources policies, and training curricula.

The tone of these employee meetings must be positive and exciting. You're describing how employees will share in the company's prosperity, gain more empowerment to make improvements, and work in an outstanding environment.

Policies and Procedures:
Establishing the Rules

POLICIES ARE A VALUABLE and necessary tool available to management. The secret is not to install excessive policies; be sure that the policies truly reinforce the company's values. The policies must be rooted in the company's values and should help guide employees' decisions and actions. Policies and procedures establish consistency and are a vehicle for controlling tasks and behavior.

| Strategic Formula |
| Company's Values |
| Policies & Procedures |
| Management Practices |
| Human Systems |
| Employee Practices |

Values-based, highly empowered, continuous-improvement cultures require far more than just the enforcement of rules. They thrive on good judgment and common sense. Excessive rules tend to stifle continuous improvement. They create the appearance of bureaucracy and management rigidity. This can reduce employee enthusiasm and the hunger for improving the enterprise. Excessive rules are as detrimental as excessive employee discretion. Seek the optimum balance between the prevalence of rules and values for your specific situation.

Policies Are Rules, So Be Careful

Excessive policies will also impede employee empowerment. Numerous companies have policy manuals that are several inches thick. After being handed a six-pound policy manual, you may have thought, "My God, there are a lot of rules here!" Or, how about that training class on the company's policies that lasted much of the day? By the afternoon, you were thinking, "I reviewed so many policies I can't remember any of them. Wow, these people sure love their policies." Policies are a great and vital management tool—just do not overuse the tool.

Keep Policies Simple, Understandable, and Accessible

Few of us take the time to read a company's entire policy manual. The nature of policy manuals makes them a boring and difficult read. This is why a company must review its key policies in new-hire orientation and require managers to attend training. If your policies are not simple and easily understandable, employees and managers will not bother to read or remember them. Employees and managers frequently inquire into specific policies only when the situation necessitates clarification. The manager will call Human Resources and ask, "What is our policy on this or that?"

In general, the thicker the policy manual, the fewer people will open it. Thus, write concise policies and keep the number of policies to a minimum. Place the policies on the company's intranet or the Internet so employees can access them from their PCs or from terminals you set up in a common area. When modifying policies, communicate the changes by highlighting them. Managers and employees will seldom read the entire document in search of the latest change.

Policies Can Work against the Company

Don't have policies for the sake of having policies. Obsolete policies that don't reflect actual practices can work against a company, particularly in legal proceedings. If a company's practices don't match a given policy, a court may hold the company to the policy even though it's no longer followed.

Courts and governmental institutions are rules-based and tend to see the world through that filter, occasionally overriding good judgment and common sense.

Utilize policies to specify what the company mandates, not to list its every desire. For example, in your policy governing one-on-one meetings between the manager and employee, don't state that these meetings are mandatory. Rather, state that supervisors are encouraged to hold at least one one-on-one meeting with their employees per quarter. Further, purge those legacy policies that have become obsolete.

Don't Let Policies Stop the Right Decision

Do not be a slave to the policy. When strict application of a policy does not match the policy's intent, use proper judgment to make the correct decision. Policies can provide a convenient excuse for managers not to labor for the needed improvement. They may say, "We can't make this or that change, because the policy says . . ." Encourage them to investigate if there is enough flexibility in the practice of the policy to accomplish the objective. Moreover, the manager or employee may need to lobby for the policy to be modified.

Every Human Resources policy should derive from a given company value. Begin each policy by describing its intent. The details of the policy should never get in the way of its general intent. State the intent of the policy at the top of each documented policy. An example of an intent statement follows.

Intent Statement for Microchip's Confidentiality Policy
Since Microchip believes that "Communication Is Vital" [*stated company value*], our employees are encouraged to have a broad knowledge of and access to products, processes, customers, and other proprietary and confidential information. In order to maintain our competitive standing in the marketplace, we expect our employees to respect and keep the confidentiality of that information. In addition, as we are a public company, it is imperative

that employees not communicate sensitive business information to anyone outside the Company.

Dangers of Excessive Discretion

Excessive discretion is where employees are over-empowered and are allowed, or decide, to use too much discretion. For example, a supervisor decides not to record the employee's actual hours worked on the time card as required by the attendance policy. The supervisor has the employee working odd hours, so the supervisor concludes that it would be easier for everyone if the employee just filled out the time card as if he worked the standard shift (8:00 A.M. to 5:00 P.M., Monday through Friday).

For fourteen months, this arrangement has seemed satisfactory. However, Human Resources now receives complaints from other employees that this employee is consistently leaving early. After an investigation, it is determined that the employee is indeed failing to work the assigned hours, leaving early several times each week. When confronted with the violation, the employee denies the accusation. The employee says, "I work my assigned hours. Look, my supervisor does not have me even logging the actual hours I work anyway."

When asked, the supervisor says, "That's true. To make everyone's life easier, I just have this employee record that he worked the standard day shift. This way, the payroll department does not get confused and I don't have to remember the precise hours the employee starts and finishes his shift. Nevertheless, I surely did not imply that the employee could leave early. Everyone must put in a full shift!"

The supervisor's excessive discretion and lack of attention have increased the difficulty of holding the employee accountable. Since the actual hours worked are not accurately reflected on the time card, as required by policy, it cannot be used to verify the accusations. To reduce excessive discretion, clarify to managers how much discretion they can exercise on each policy. If they exceed this level of discretion, hold them personally accountable.

Train Employees Up Front

You must train employees on the appropriate policies as part of your new-hire orientation class. Further, managers must receive in-depth training on understanding and interpreting the policies. When acquiring a company, train the employees on the company's culture and policies as soon as possible. New employees need to know the values and rules of the company in order to perform properly. Tell the employees why you have the policies as you explain their intended purpose.

Certain Policies Are Required by Law or for Safety

Certain policies are required by law or are necessary to maintain a safe environment. Therefore, enforcement of these policies allows for little deviation. For example, no latitude should be granted to employees to breach the fire alarm policy or to ignore discrimination laws surrounding interviewing and hiring.

16

Management Practices

MANAGERS FIRST AND FOREMOST must role model the company's values and policies. The management practices must align with the company's values. The entire *Aggregate System* breaks down if too many managers serve as anti-role models of the company's culture. It's imperative that management practices what it preaches and leads by example. Employees won't practice the company's values if their bosses don't. Managers who practice the firm's values influence others to do so.

Second, managers must assist employees in their practice of the company's values while conducting company business. Managers must foster the expectation that employees act in accordance with the company's values. Moreover, they need to hold the employees accountable for practicing those values. Every business should value and demand excellent performance from each employee. Strong management skills are essential in a values-based, highly empowered environment. The manager must find that balance point between empowering employees and providing adequate coaching.

189

Employee empowerment requires considerable communication between management and employees. Empowered cultures are dynamic environments with many employees striving to make improvements. It's critical for everyone to be on the same page. Ongoing coaching helps employees learn how to use proper judgment and to solve problems. You can't learn things such as judgment by just attending a course. Employees should become stronger performers as they're coached through each assignment. Furthermore, to maximize employees' performance, managers must tailor their management style to each employee's abilities and personality. The theory that there's a single best management style is long gone.

The 25 Desired Characteristics of Managers and Supervisors

The role of managers and supervisors in instituting and preserving the desired company culture is commonly underestimated. Many firms place insufficient weight on the true impact of managers and supervisors. This is reflected in their hiring, training, promotion, assessment, and employee-recognition practices. In reality, the managers' management styles and abilities have a tremendous impact on the company's culture and performance. Underrating their influence will significantly decrease the effectiveness of your *Aggregate System*.

Figure 16.1 lists the 25 desired characteristics of managers and supervisors. This list illustrates how difficult it is to be an outstanding manager. It requires considerable commitment and training to become an excellent manager. Seldom will any given manager possess all 25 characteristics. Therefore, companies will benefit from a comprehensive management development curriculum. The company should use these 25 desired characteristics as the basis for its hiring criteria, job descriptions, performance appraisals, promotional criteria, and training classes.

All too often, firms rate managers on their personality or ability to get results independent of the damage to employees. They would benefit from rating managers based on their mastery of the 25 desired characteristics. If employees work for a manager with a good personality, they're content.

1. Achieves the desired operational performance goals; consistently meets commitments and demands quality.
2. Displays professionalism and role models the culture.
3. Has technical competence in his/her field.
4. Drives continuous improvement.
5. Is bright and has good common sense.
6. Seeks to satisfy customers (internal and external).
7. Demonstrates excellent people skills and interpersonal interactions.
8. Practices a dynamic leadership style (i.e., situational leadership); serves as a coach, facilitator, and barrier remover.
9. Empowers employees to foster their involvement, getting the most from them.
10. Has solid performance management skills (e.g., establishes expectations, demonstrates conflict resolution skills, and deals with nonperformers).
11. Has good judgment and decision-making abilities; takes appropriate risks.
12. Demonstrates initiative, is a creative problem solver, and utilizes analytical methods.
13. Is a strong communicator with good selling, persuasion, and negotiating skills.
14. Is a dedicated, hard worker who demonstrates initiative, perseverance, and follow-through.
15. Is flexible and adaptable and works well under stress.
16. Fosters continuous learning by developing employees.
17. Is a good organizer and planner, with a systems orientation.
18. Listens actively and considers others' input and feedback.
19. Gives recognition for good work, takes interest in the individual, and remains focused on the work rather than playing politics.
20. Is a team player who builds good team chemistry, is a consensus builder, but knows when to lead.
21. Respects, praises, and supports other groups rather than seeking control over them.
22. Operates with limited ego; acts ethically and honestly.
23. Is a good motivator who effectively deals with poor performers.
24. Is frugal (i.e., profit and loss/cost sensitivity).
25. Is concerned with maintaining a safe workplace.

FIGURE 16.1: The 25 Desired Characteristics of Managers and Supervisors

If not, they end up not liking their job. It's common for employees to struggle with the personality of their boss. The number one reason people leave companies is that they dislike their boss.

Strong Management Skills

A values-based, highly empowered, continuous-improvement environment demands strong managerial skills. Managers can't be experts on everything. Nor can they just tell people what to do or closely monitor everyone's adherence to the rules. The environment is too dynamic when everyone's empowered. Chapter 8 described the various management styles that impede the culture. Coaching and developing employees requires considerable interaction with the employee. The manager's effectiveness is reduced if he or she lacks proficient people-management and interpersonal skills.

Sometimes, becoming an exceptional manager requires the conviction to set aside one's psychological needs and personality traits. For example, let's say that the operation is staffed with good employees and is running quite well. However, the manager enjoys constantly being in the middle of the action so he or she can demonstrate his or her problem-solving abilities. This is what makes the job interesting. But the real question is, "Would the organization be better off if the manager focused more on developing his or her employees' ability to problem solve rather than fulfilling his or her own needs?" The answer is, "Yes." Having an organization with several individuals with good judgment and the ability to solve problems is more beneficial in the long run. It's difficult for us to put our needs aside for the good of our subordinates. In fact, it may make us feel more insecure because we feel less valuable to the company.

Contingent Management Style

As the science of business management has evolved, so has its vision of the ideal management style. Over the last fifty years the perceived role of the manager has taken many shapes. The academic field has searched for the ideal management style. They have presented everything from auto-cratic managers to managers at the dot-com firms, with their "give your employees total freedom and even let them bring their dog to work" man-agement styles.

No single management style is most effective. Rather, the most effec-tive style is one that adapts to the particular situation. Managers customize their style to the employees and prevailing circumstances, as opposed to the traditional approach of forcing the employees to adapt to a manager's style. So the most effective management style is not a style, it's a general approach to managing others, one that changes in order to optimize an em-ployee's performance based on ability and the job at hand.

Ken Blanchard has popularized this approach through his Situational Leadership programs. He has managers tailor their management style based on employees' task maturity (i.e., their ability to independently com-plete the assigned task) and their need for interaction with their manager. His approach and programs are excellent.

A contingent management style is important in an empowered envi-ronment. For example, if you give too much direction, people feel over-controlled and irritated. On the other hand, if individuals are given too little direction based on their ability, they become anxious or frustrated. Also, if you misjudge their relationship needs they may feel unfulfilled, in-secure, or nervous.

The perceived role of the manager has also evolved over the years. Tra-ditionally, the manager's role was to plan, organize, and maintain tight con-trol over employees. Today, managers are less focused on micromanaging and act more as coaches, facilitators, developers, and leaders as circum-stances dictate.

When Executives and Managers Become Anti-Role Models

What's the correct course of action when executives or managers don't practice the company's values? What should happen when, in fact, some managers may even be serving as anti-role models? In Chapter 8 we dis-cussed several management styles that can serve as anti-role models to the desired culture. Every firm eventually faces this situation with some of their managers. The success of your culture may rest on how effectively you resolve such occurrences. Chapter 11 detailed the process for resolving these types of situations.

Figure 16.2 illustrates that an individual's practice of the company's values can be expressed using a normal distribution. Some individuals will practice the values more often than the average of the employee population. Other individuals will practice the values less often.

The more senior and visible the position the anti-role model individual occupies in the organization, the greater the negative impact. This is where the CEO and/or executives must take a stand. The corrective action is straightforward. Tell the individual the specific behaviors and instances that indicate there's a problem. Discuss which company value or policy the

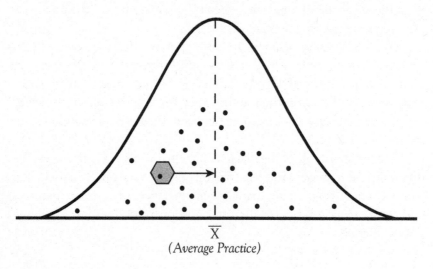

$$\overline{X}$$
(Average Practice)

- • = Executives and Managers
- ⬡ = Anti-Role Model Executive or Manager

Goal: At a minimum, persuade, or, if necessary, pressure the individual into giving the impression that he/she believes in the company's values

Figure 16.2: Dealing with Anti-Role Model Executives and Managers

person is violating. Set clear expectations and devise a plan to correct the individual's weaknesses. In addition to coaching the individual, involve Human Resources and the Training group if necessary.

The objective is to convince the individual who is acting as the anti-role model to embrace the firm's values and begin role modeling them. Sometimes the person is not able, or is unwilling, to modify the undesirable personality trait or management style. If the individual's value to the operation still outweighs his or her negative impact, you nevertheless need to take action. The weakness principle discussed in Chapter 10 is at play here. The individual has strong strengths (skills) and strong weaknesses. At a minimum, persuade—or, if necessary, pressure—the individual into giving the impression to other employees that he or she is practicing the culture. The goal becomes to reduce such people's negative influence for the time being. Make them neutral influences rather than anti-role models.

Do the Best Performers Make the Best Managers?

Firms frequently promote employees into manager positions because they're the strongest performer or the most technical member of the group. This approach is fine if the individual is competent in a sufficient number of the 25 desired characteristics of managers or has a sincere commitment to master them. However, this is often not the case. The unfortunate subordinates are saddled with a manager who possesses marginal management skills. We've all directly or indirectly witnessed this scenario.

The sporting world learned this lesson long ago. Rarely are former superstars hired as managers or coaches. They typically gained stardom by focusing inward. They are gifted with amazing skills and driven to outwork and outplay the other guy. As coaches they can't understand why the players don't work harder, why they don't play up to the former superstars' expectations.

With their inward focus, superstars commonly fail to learn the little things, those things that many less-gifted athletes learned, such as how to listen, the mechanics of the game, effectively interacting and influencing people, cheering the other guy on, patience, and humility.

Avoid the temptation to automatically promote the highest performer or most technically proficient individual. Look for the person who has a natural aptitude for managing others, the individual who has worked to acquire managerial skills, someone who gets pleasure out of helping others succeed. Make sure your human systems (see Chapter 17) promote and train the individuals best suited to manage others.

The Power of Likeability, Respect, and Trust

The top reasons people change jobs are that they don't like, respect, and/or trust their manager. Therefore, it's important that managers master the likeability factor. You don't get your employees to like and respect you by giving them whatever they want, going easy on them, or being overly friendly. A manager earns respect by displaying professionalism, demonstrating excellent interpersonal and communication skills, and taking an interest in the individual.

We more readily forgive and overlook weakness in managers we like. If we dislike a manager we seem to look for behaviors that reinforce our perception of that person. Un-likeability is hard to overcome. Moving a subordinate from dislike to like requires a considerable effort on the manager's part. Politicians know the disastrous effects of un-likeability. This is why they measure their likeability and un-likeability in their polling.

Human Systems:
Backbone of the Culture

FOR THE AGGREGATE SYSTEM to succeed and become self-perpetuating, the human systems must be designed to ensure a company's values, policies, management practices, and employees are aligned. This alignment is critical. The *human systems* are the systems the company uses to organize, staff, communicate, assess, recognize, compensate, develop, and advance employees. These systems are illustrated in Figure 17.1. They directly touch the employees, either reinforcing the desired culture or tearing it apart. Each subsystem that comprises the human systems must integrate with the other systems so that employees do not receive mixed signals on what the company desires from them.

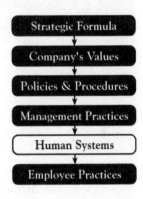

These systems, which tell employees what the firm actually values and rewards, influence employee decisions and actions from the day they're hired to the day they leave the company. They let the employees know if the company is honestly practicing what it preaches. For example, do the employees in fact share in the company's prosperity? Are employees in truth empowered to work with others to make improvements? Does the

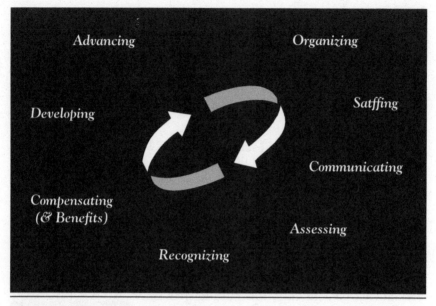

Advancing

Organizing

Developing

Satffing

Communicating

Compensating
(& Benefits)

Assessing

Recognizing

FIGURE 17.1: Human Systems: Systems Designed to Ensure the Company's Values,
Policies, Management Practices, and Employees Are Aligned

company care about the employees' development and careers? Does the
company evaluate employees' performance against what they say they
want? How much communication do employees actually receive?

Michael recalls a company in which the human systems were not
aligned with the management practices. The senior management consistently articulated the virtues of teamwork. In meetings with employees,
the senior managers routinely expressed the importance of being a team
player. "It's a new day, we all have to work as one, we all need to pull on the
same side of the rope," they'd say, with an apparent evangelistic commitment. They even began introducing the next speaker on the agenda as,
"My teammate, so and so." Yes, it seemed a little over the top to Michael,
too. Kirk Johnston, seated next to Michael at one of these meetings, was
a graduate of Stanford University. Kirk had been with the company for
eleven years in the Product Engineering group. Leaning over, he quietly
commented, "What company do *they* work for?"

As Michael and Kirk watched, the senior managers were shaking each other's hands and referring to one another as teammate. No one had the courage, or perhaps the foolishness, to point out that other than these speeches praising fellow teammates, there was a distinct absence of teamwork across the enterprise. You couldn't find examples of teamwork even if you made a concerted effort. Well, at least the teammate behavior by senior management was a curiosity to witness. Sometimes it's fascinating to watch such a contrast between management's perception of a company's practice and that of the employees. Michael and Kirk took the whole thing in stride; this wasn't the first company not to practice what it preached. At least the meeting adjourned on time, so they headed back to the refuge of their cubicles.

At lunch the following day, Michael dined in the cafeteria with six fellow employees. As they consumed their usual entrées, the conversation evolved into a discussion surrounding the utter absence of teamwork at the firm. This topic was still fresh on their minds since senior management's meeting with all the employees the previous afternoon. They each took turns sarcastically restating the platitudes on teamwork that senior management had expressed. Jim Comings, from the Finance group, initiated the conversation by saying, "Remember guys, it's a new day, we all have to work as one." Then Kevin Blake, from the Quality group, chimed in, saying, "Let's not forget to pull on the same side of the rope." The guys at the table chuckled. By now, everyone at the table had become somewhat silly, referring to each other as teammate. These types of sarcastic conversations commonly occur when the stated practices don't reflect reality.

As the conversation turned more serious, Michael and his lunchmates wondered why, if senior management truly wanted teamwork, the human systems didn't reflect this desire. For example, the organizational structures were solidly functional in nature, even to the point that crossfunctional teams were discouraged. The prevailing feeling was that "we don't discuss issues outside the group" and "we will fix our part of the problem and the others will resolve theirs."

It seemed that everyone was attempting to cover their backsides, shifting the blame down- or upstream. The quandary was that many of the operational problems stemmed from circumstances that crossed functional lines, or were a result of transition points between functions. Moreover, no one communicated with each other, surely not on how these transition points could be strengthened. Doing so might suggest that they were experiencing a problem with another group, potentially initiating a political battle within senior management. These conflicts were to be avoided, unless you held all the cards or had a winning hand.

If teamwork was vital, why were the cash bonuses based solely on an individual's efforts, reflecting no team accomplishments? And why were there no training classes on teamwork? Why wasn't teamwork emphasized on the employees' annual performance appraisal? Worst of all, team players were seldom promoted into management positions. The hard-driving, high-ego person who believed in survival of the fittest or "my project must succeed at all costs" was always the one who got the opportunity to lead others. After analyzing and solving the company's problems, Michael and the other employees dropped the remnants of their lunches in the trash, placed their trays on the counter, and ventured back to their cubicles.

The human systems have another important function besides ensuring that the company's values, policies, management practices, and employees are aligned. They play a primary role in fostering the desired core personality characteristics the company expects from employees. Included are such things as being a team player, striving for the highest quality, meeting commitments, keeping customers satisfied, solving problems, and endeavoring to make improvements to the operation. Naturally, even with an excellent staffing system, not all employees who join the company display these core characteristics. Nevertheless, if the human systems continually reinforce these desired characteristics, over time, their practice will become more pervasive.

The Organizing System

The *organizing system* includes processes or systems that are used to design (1) the various operations, (2) the organizational structure required to obtain the operational objectives, and (3) the individual positions within the organization. The goal of the organizing system is to organize the operation and jobs to achieve excellence in quality, costs, cycle times, customer satisfaction, and continuous improvement and innovation. Today's workforce is expected to multitask, completing a widening span of tasks within the employee's field of expertise.

Teams of people, rather than isolated individuals, are tackling problem-resolution and improvement activities. Typically, these teams will consist of employees from several different organizational areas. What these cross-functional team members have in common is that they all play an interrelated role in managing a specific part of the operation. Since individuals still drive a significant portion of the continuous-improvement activity in any organization, it's crucial that employee empowerment be incorporated into the job-design process. Today, jobs must be designed with flexible boundaries. The days of "that's not my job" are long gone.

It's best to avoid placing too much emphasis on formal job descriptions. They can encourage the formation of undesirable boundaries surrounding an individual's job responsibilities, and this will impede continuous-improvement efforts. To be useful, a job description needs to be specific. However, detailed job descriptions soon become outdated because employees' roles are constantly changing, while supervisors and Human Resources have too little time to continually update them. To make up for this, companies attempt to make the descriptions more general. However, when the descriptions become too general, they no longer add value. It's a vicious cycle.

We prefer to use job assignments rather than job descriptions. In fact, we design performance appraisals to begin with the supervisor stating the employee's job assignments, rather than the formal job description. This technique avoids any potential debate with the employee concerning the true job description. If you document an employee's job assignments within a performance appraisal, the focus will remain on what the employee was asked to do rather than on a theoretical job description.

The Staffing System

The *Aggregate System* requires an effective *staffing system*, the system by which the organization hires prospective candidates. The goal of this system is to hire employees with the correct expertise and desired core personality characteristics. When a company is staffing, the criteria it uses to select new employees are critical. Figure 16.1 shows the 25 desired characteristics of managers and supervisors. Chapter 19 describes the 18 desired characteristics of employees, shown in Figure 19.3. The core characteristics provided in Figure 16.1 and Figure 19.3 can serve as a starting point for you to develop your specific selection criteria. In general, the selection criteria should mirror the criteria used for assessing employees and determining promotions. If these criteria become too divergent, the *Aggregate System* will become misaligned.

It's always advantageous for candidates to interview with several employees because the group-interviewing process increases the probability that the correct decision will be reached. This interviewing team should consist of the supervisor, peers, an individual representing internal customers, and Human Resources. It's important to make sure you develop questions and techniques to assess the candidate's personality characteristics. Some interviewers should specifically focus on assessing if the candidate will embrace the company's stated values and performance expectations. After the interviews are completed, the group can select the best candidate for the position. If you have a candidate who will be a great hire but doesn't interview well, you'll benefit from coaching that candidate before the interviews.

You should have an in-depth conversation with the candidate in which you describe the company's culture and sell the candidate on the company. Show the candidate the results of your employee survey on the company culture and overall job satisfaction. Provide the applicant with literature on the company and show the results of the company's quarterly and annual performance. Remember, you'll either hire employees who need lots of maintenance or employees who find solutions, so take the time to get it right.

Always strive to fill positions from employees within the company. These individuals already know the company culture and hopefully have a proven track record. If no candidates from within the organization are available, a great method for finding prospective candidates is to institute an internal referrals program, which gives employees an incentive to refer candidates they know could do the job.

The Communication System

We cannot overstate the importance of maintaining an excellent communication system within a values-based, highly empowered, continuous-improvement culture. The *communication system* is the system, or structure, by which formalized communication is exchanged. Its foundation lies in the value the company places on honest, free-flowing communication between organizational functions and individuals. If the company desires an abundance of free-flowing communication, then the communication system will be elaborate. If the company doesn't emphasize communication, the system may be quite brief and simple. Empowering cultures distribute authority; thus, communication is essential to understanding and carrying out the company's objectives. It's critical that everyone be on the same page. If empowered employees lack key information, don't know what their managers expect from them, or don't know that conditions have changed, they may make incorrect decisions.

The communication system should be built around the fact that the company embraces the virtues associated with communication. It should consist of components installed to satisfy the various communication requirements. Here are some of the components that constitute a comprehensive communication system that Microchip has found to be effective:

- Regularly scheduled one-on-one meetings with supervisors and employees
- Weekly or monthly staff meetings
- Monthly or quarterly departmental meetings
- Quarterly communication meetings from the CEO to all employees
- Formal employee luncheons with senior management
- Employee meetings with senior management that utilize the open door policy
- Project reviews
- Periodic operational reviews
- Weekly booking and billing meetings
- Quarterly management by objectives (MBOs) or Vital Few activities

- Various reports
- Company newsletters

These components are essential for providing methods by which the enterprise's employees can communicate effectively and efficiently. Each component is designed to address a specific communication need. For example, employee one-on-one meetings ensure that employee and supervisor routinely dedicate time to communicate. During these meetings, the supervisor can monitor the employee's work; update the employee on changes to strategies, priorities, or business conditions; and discuss the employee's performance. Figure 17.2 shows a form Microchip developed to be used by managers to prepare for a one-on-one meeting with an employee.

The employee one-on-one meetings are also an opportunity for employees to discuss any subject of concern (scheduling vacations, issues that

---

Employee's Name:
Supervisor's Name:
Date:

Policy No: HR 420
Issue Date: 09-30-91
Revised: 01-15-94

Agenda   Notes

Personal Issues:

Work Issues:

Project Updates:
(Review Schedules)

Improvements:

Source: Microchip Technology

FIGURE 17.2: Microchip's One-on-One Form

they are having with other employees, family difficulties affecting their performance, or dislike of the supervisor's management style). As you can see in Figure 17.2, any personal issues the employee may wish to discuss appear first on the one-on-one agenda. Often managers and employees tend to concentrate on work issues and project updates and leave personal issues till the end of the meeting. Since time is limited, if you don't put personal issues first, they will likely not be addressed. Rather, they tend to be deferred until a subsequent meeting.

The employee one-on-one meeting ensures there are no surprises on the employee's annual performance appraisal—any concerns about the employee's performance should have been discussed in the meetings. The performance appraisal is the summary of the employee's accomplishments and development efforts, as discussed during the employee's regularly scheduled one-on-one meetings.

Remember what's key is that the company sincerely values and practices honest, open, and free-flowing communication throughout the enterprise. The communication system is constructed on this premise. A communication system will probably be weak if the company is doing just the bare minimum, or if it installs components within the communication system only because the employees are demanding more communication. You'll know the system is working when nobody even thinks about it, as it has become a part of everyday life.

When constructing its communication system, a company should consider the physical mechanisms by which communication will transpire. I know this seems obvious. However, we've worked for firms that lacked sufficient conference rooms to foster a team environment. Further, many companies still lack video conferencing capabilities between their main sites. Here are some of the various physical mechanisms by which communication is carried out:

- Meeting rooms
- Phones, including cell phones
- PCs
- Memos and documents
- E-mail

- Videotaping
- Video conferencing
- Company-wide intranet
- Internet (such as Webcast presentations)

The CEO's Quarterly Employee Communication Meeting Is the Single Most Powerful Vehicle for Instilling and Maintaining the Company's Culture

The CEO's quarterly employee communication meeting has a number of functions. This meeting, which takes place at the end of each quarter, allows employees to hear how the company is doing directly from the top. In addition, time is set aside for employees to ask questions, during which they can see if the CEO practices the company culture or not. Typically, this meeting focuses on how the company is performing overall, market conditions, quarterly P&L results, stock performance, major initiatives, and current challenges. Moreover, during such meetings, variable compensation payouts, such as company-wide employee bonuses, are discussed. When the company experiences a difficult period, such meetings are effective forums to discuss the situation. If the company has had to shut down a factory or conduct a layoff, for instance, the CEO can explain the action. This may scare some CEOs, but having seen it done on several occasions, we can testify to its advantages. If the CEO is open and forthright, employees love these meetings.

The meetings also reinforce that communication is valued. You'll often hear employees say after these meetings, "With such a hectic schedule, isn't it great that the CEO takes the time to communicate with us directly?" This is the CEO's time to reach the people and inspire them to achieve future goals, or to prepare them to begin adapting to difficult business conditions. It may be impractical for the CEO to talk to all employees face to face. Therefore, technology may be needed to conduct the meeting. For example, the CEO can give a live meeting to a large group of employees at one site and then video- or phone-conference the other sites. You can utilize the Internet if desired. Employees who work on the off-shifts or at satellite locations can watch the meeting on videotape.

Many CEOs will initiate these meetings with a sincere desire to improve communication. However, due to the demand placed on the CEO, often these types of meetings will get postponed and somehow never get rescheduled. Soon, other pressing problems come up. Then the business environment may change and the CEO will no longer clearly know whether the following quarter will be a good one or the start of a downturn. The CEO then avoids facing the employees and cancels another quarterly employee communication meeting. By now nine months may have gone by and regular communication meetings have become a thing of the past.

Conducting regular quarterly employee communication meetings requires a true and honest commitment from the CEO. At Microchip, Steve has not missed a quarterly communication meeting with the employees since July of 1990. We have always felt that during times of transition, it is even more important to have communication meetings with employees. In January 2005, it was not clear which way the semiconductor industry was headed. Some Wall Street analysts believed the industry was headed downward. Other analysts and some industry executives felt that it would be a short-lived inventory correction. Steve, in his January 2005 communication meeting with employees, discussed this situation in detail. He discussed his position, opposing views concerning the future market conditions, a series of "what if" scenarios, and Microchip's strategy and back-up plans. Steve left employees with specific instructions to be frugal and cut back on discretionary expenses. He also laid out a plan for future growth irrespective of the short-term direction of the industry.

The response from the employees was overwhelmingly positive. Here are two e-mails from employees that typify the employees' appreciation with Steve's open and honest communication:

Mr. Sanghi,

I just thought you would like to know that today's quarterly communication meeting was more educational than any business class I have ever attended . . . Thank you.

Regards,
Jeff

Steve,

I wanted to provide you with some positive feedback that I have received from the Production Specialists on our most recent quarterly communications meeting. The people were extremely pleased with your honesty. They felt you provided them with clear-cut information on where we stand as a company, while still preparing them for any negative actions that could come up. They felt you showed that you gave thoughtful consideration for the employees and company as a whole. Many of the people strongly agreed with your accuracy about our trends, directions, and the good judgment you have delivered over the years. I believe you made an excellent impression on the employees and have effectively gained their support with your current decision.

Thank you,
Sheila

Formal CEO Luncheons with Employees

Another important meeting a CEO (or a senior manager) should have is formal luncheons with employees. Andrew Grove, former CEO of Intel, often referred to these as "bunch for lunch." The concept is to take a semi-random group of employees and invite them to lunch with the CEO. It is semi-random to the point that you want a mix of managers, engineers, factory employees, people responsible for administrative tasks, and so on. You also want to choose the employees from within those areas randomly. This should ensure that a cross section of the employee population is selected. The purpose of the lunches is for the CEO to get to know the employees in a more personal setting. But it's not a social affair. The topic of discussion allows the CEO to obtain direct feedback from a random group of employees regarding what is happening in the trenches. You can gauge morale, the level of communication within the company, and the employees' concerns from these lunches.

These lunches are especially helpful after a CEO's quarterly communication meeting, as previously described. This allows the CEO to judge the effectiveness of the quarterly employee communication meetings and gauge how well the message was received and understood. A word of caution, though: don't expect the employees to open up right away. Some will be intimidated, but others will open up and break the ice. It's especially difficult to start these luncheons after the announcement of bad news. So, you have to build these luncheons as part of your culture of communication.

The Importance of an Open Door Policy

An *open door policy* is a company-wide policy that allows all employees to bring any issue to anyone in their management chain or to Human Resources. Employees are encouraged to escalate the issue up the organizational hierarchy within their management chain of command until the issue is addressed. For example, if an employee were in Manufacturing and couldn't find a satisfactory resolution to an issue, the employee would eventually get an audience with the Vice President of Manufacturing or even the CEO. Employees can utilize the identical process in the Human Resources management chain. If an employee felt uncomfortable bringing an issue to anyone but the Vice President of Human Resources or the CEO, he or she could have direct access to either party. This would apply to issues such as sexual harassment or inappropriate conduct within the employee's management hierarchy.

When implementing this policy, some managers feel apprehensive at first. They worry that the employees may abuse the policy, taking all their issues directly to senior management and bypassing them. This concern is understandable. However, our experience is that this concern is unfounded. Rarely do employees want to bring their issue to senior management if it's not required. The benefits of maintaining the desired culture clearly outweigh the occasional abuse. Human Resources is there to ensure that the proper escalation process, through the management hierarchy, is being followed. If management truly embraces this policy, it strongly reinforces the company's commitment to communication. It also gives a voice to those employees who need to be heard. With an open door policy, the answer the employees receive is often not what they want to hear. However, the employees typically appreciate that management cared enough to listen. This type of open access to management builds a great deal of good will between management and the employees. In addition, it can keep the company out of legal problems if potential violations were not addressed.

Communication, in general, takes on different dynamics based on where one lies in the corporate hierarchy. For example, if the CEO wants to implement an initiative, it will get articulated directly to the executive management. Therefore, the executive management possess a clear understanding of what needs to change and the rationale behind it. The objective is known and understood. Problems arise, however, when executive management pass on their version of the objective to mid-level managers, assuming it'll get communicated throughout the enterprise.

For mid-level managers, the new initiative represents only one of many activities they're attempting to communicate and execute. The mid-level managers are also receiving a countless number of upward communications from the employees who are actually doing the work. They are caught in the middle, and are often overwhelmed with information and initiatives. What makes it worse is that most companies have adopted a flat organizational structure that requires fewer mid-level managers. Mid-level managers are constantly receiving intense multidirectional communication, not to mention countless phone calls and e-mails they haven't gotten to yet. This is often where the communication process breaks down. You might even hear a manager say to the employee, "I'm not sure why we need to do this, but just get it done." The rationale and expectations associated with the objective that the CEO clearly stated have lost their clarity. This is not necessarily the fault of mid-level management—they're often truly overloaded.

The employees, who are individual contributors, are left to complete the objective. The employees may not care about the importance of the initiative, since no one has communicated it to them. Not having all the information necessary, many employees will become passive. Instead of aggressively executing the objective, they take on a wait and see or "it's not my job" mind-set. The employees will not enthusiastically tackle the activity since they're uncomfortable with the amount of communication they received. In such a case, these employees' efforts are far from being optimized. It's apparent that excellent communication, especially at the mid-manager level, requires commitment and a concerted effort. In order to ensure corporate objectives are clearly communicated, management must find avenues to enhance communication between all levels of the enterprise.

The Assessment System

The purpose of the assessment system is to evaluate employees' performance. We must evaluate employees to determine how we are going to rate them, compared to their peers for the purpose of compensation. Assessment is the first step in fostering an employee's development or continuous improvement. Employees need to understand the criteria by which they're being assessed and management's expectations. In a continuous-improvement culture, it's mandatory that the employees continuously enhance their expertise and abilities. In addition, supervisors need to assess how the employee is impacting the operation. Moreover, tasks performed by people often constitute a large part of the operational process. Therefore, optimizing the operation frequently involves optimizing the abilities of the employees.

Many methods and tools are available for assessing employees. (There is an abundance of literature on these methods and tools, so we will not conduct a comprehensive review.) Assessment tools include analysis of personality styles, surveys, focus groups, productivity measures, interviews, 360-degree assessments, management luncheons with employees, and the traditional annual performance appraisal. The assessment tool that influences employee performance the most is the performance appraisal. Although performance appraisals are the most frequently used assessment tool, they are commonly misused. Therefore, we have devoted an entire chapter, Chapter 18, to this subject.

The Recognition System

It's important to recognize employee accomplishments because doing so satisfies a basic human need—the need for other people to acknowledge our individuality and appreciate our worthy actions. If you fail to satisfy this need, employees will find the culture to be somewhat empty. This doesn't mean they'll leave the company solely because they never get recognized or appreciated. However, you will lose out because recognizing employees could have a profound impact on your company. It's foolish not to have a culture that recognizes and appreciates employees, as the costs associated with this system are minimal. Most people will be satisfied with receiving informal forms of recognition such as a sincere thank you or a bit of praise. So, create a culture that acknowledges and appreciates people and their contributions.

The recognition system should also consist of formal vehicles to acknowledge people's hard work. These types of honors are well known to all Human Resources professionals. They include employee of the month awards and plaques. If teamwork is important to your organization's success, ensure that you also recognize team achievements.

Individual and team excellence must be given both public and private recognition. Be careful that the employees don't perceive the mechanisms by which they are recognized as divisive or trite. For example, if the same employees, or teams, are consistently being recognized, this can lead to resentment.

Giving a lot of little forms of recognition can be more effective than infrequent, larger awards. Utilize small awards such as dinner coupons, movie tickets, free soda, on-site barbecues, recognition luncheons in the cafeteria, and the like to let employees know you recognize their contributions.

The Compensation and Benefits Systems

As with all the subsystems that comprise the human systems, it's critical that the compensation and benefits systems be designed to reinforce the desired culture and foster the core personality characteristics you expect employees to demonstrate. In the *Aggregate System*, compensation is merit based, utilizing a variable compensation approach, while emphasizing an employee's total compensation package.

Merit-based compensation means that employees are compensated based on the merits of their performance. For the purpose of determining an employee's salary increases and other related compensation, that employee's performance and value to the operation are compared with those of other individuals within the employee's peer group. Employees within the peer group are then ranked in descending order, ratings are assigned, and salary increases are determined. This process is utilized to ensure that increases to compensation are based on the merit of one's performance within the group.

Variable compensation means that some of the components of an employee's total compensation are tied to the company's performance. For example, all Microchip employees are eligible to receive a quarterly cash bonus if the company achieves specific quarterly results. If the company achieves its criteria, employees receive the bonus at the conclusion of the quarter. If the performance of the company falls short, due to poor execution or a down business cycle, no bonus is awarded.

The variable approach has two primary objectives. First, it motivates and retains employees by allowing them to share in the company's prosperity. Second, it reduces expense pressure on the P&L in downward business cycles. There are several other forms of variable compensation, such as stock options and profit sharing (discussed in greater detail in Chapter 7). In the *Aggregate System*, a substantial portion of an employee's overall compensation can come from components other than base salary. Therefore, compensation must be viewed from the perspective of one's total compensation, rather than just one's base salary.

The overall goal should be to beat your competitors in total compensation, not on base salary. Total compensation accounts for such things as financial gains from stock options, employee stock purchase plans, cash bonuses, profit sharing, 401(k) or retirement company matching, and employee benefits.

The Employee Development System

The *employee development system* is the vehicle used to improve the performance of employees. It instills and maintains the culture, while enhancing the abilities and expertise of the employees. Additionally, the system must reinforce the core personality characteristics the company expects of its employees and managers. It typically consists of the Human Resources, Training, or Organizational Development (OD) departments. The system is a crucial piece in perpetuating a continuous learning environment. It allows the company to maintain an educated, ever-improving employee population.

In the *Aggregate System*, the employee development system is used to instill those values you want to have a sense of permanence. For example, if you want a company where employees know how to manage projects, you'll require training courses on project management and time management. If teamwork is critical, then courses on team building and leading teams will be required. Companies who state they want world-class managers but don't offer training on such things as managing people have designed a system with a low probability of obtaining the stated objective.

The employee development system also works hand in hand with the annual employee performance appraisal's areas for further development. Employees may address many of their developmental areas by attending training classes or by receiving individualized coaching. Training can be expensive, so use it on the things you want to become enduring fixtures of the organization. Furthermore, when new initiatives modify or place greater emphasis on an aspect of the current culture, and you want the change to endure, add to the curriculum a course on the subject, and train all the existing employees. If the change represents a significant modification to the status quo, initially a senior manager should teach the class. This will demonstrate to the employees that management is serious about the subject. For example, if the objective is to lower manufacturing cycle times, the Vice President of Manufacturing should teach the course to the manufacturing management team. Then management can teach it to the rest of the organization.

If you're serious about the company's culture, you need to develop a course that describes the culture to new employees. This will make people more effective sooner. It is also very helpful to formally train international employees on the company's U.S. culture and vice versa, especially when a company has acquired employees through an acquisition or merger.

In addition, the employee development system increases employee job satisfaction and retention. Today's employees want to feel that they have a career path and that they are periodically enhancing their abilities. Employees are more mobile than ever. They may change companies and jobs several times during their careers. They are keenly aware that in to-day's market, real job security and increasing compensation come from one's expertise and ability to perform. Hence, people are very focused on improving their skills, and expect companies to offer training and educational services.

When recruiting candidates, you should tout your company's commitment to employee development. We've seen this, coupled with liking the prospective company's culture, to be a deciding factor for why candidates accepted positions with a company. Show the candidate your course catalog, and any honors or awards you've received that are relevant to employee development. For example, in 2001 Microchip was rated as the 18th best training organization in the nation by *Training Magazine*. This type of honor clearly demonstrates the company's commitment to employee development.

The Components of the Employee Development System

The employee development system consists of several components that all focus on strengthening the employees' expertise and abilities. It also works to enhance the effectiveness of various groups within the company. Employees increase their value to the organization when they enhance their expertise, abilities, and performance. This is analogous to the R&D expenses on your P&L. Investing in new technologies or products reduces short-term profits because you're investing in the future. In this case, the investment is in your employees' expertise. Ultimately their future contributions to the enterprise will grow.

After Microchip was recognized as the 18th best training organization in the nation, Steve was discussing training with another industry CEO, whom we will refer to as Jim Garvey. Jim said that he does not like to spend a lot of time training his people. Jim said, "Training is expensive and what happens if after receiving training the employee leaves the company?" Steve thought for a moment and asked, "Jim, what happens if you don't train your employees and they stay?" Jim was truly perplexed and could not answer the question. The moral of this exchange was not lost on Jim. Companies who don't invest in their employees' development think in only the short-term, which is not conducive to installing an *Aggregate System*.

The components that comprise the employee development system are in no way novel. The key is to design them to reinforce the culture and to attain the company's strategic formula. This really begins with your company's in-house training curriculum. It's important that the company not only maintain a comprehensive employee development system, but that it also search for ways to get employees and teams to utilize it. Some common techniques to increase utilization are ensuring that supervisors send people to classes, paying employees while they are in training courses delivered on site or when they are attending seminars, and giving recognition for completing certification programs. Some companies require individuals to complete a core set of courses, or possess equivalent knowledge, prior to being provided advancement opportunities. Here are some of the components of the employee development system:

- Company's in-house training curriculum
- Training registration, certification, and tracking programs
- Guest or outside contract instructors
- On-the-job training
- Coaching and mentoring from others in the organization
- Career development programs
- Organizational Development (OD) activities
- Learning through self-discovery
- Formal outside training courses from vendors or seminars
- College institutions
- Vocational institutions
- Memberships in associations

The Key to Making Your Employee Development System Effective

Make sure the curriculum is comprehensive and relevant to the employees' jobs and career aspirations. *Comprehensive* means having courses on all, or most, of the subjects the company determines are critical. They could be courses on design of experiments, basic statistics, project management, conflict resolution, quality methodologies, problem solving, interviewing, customer service, or whatever is determined to be important. The employee development system is effective only if managers and employees use it. Therefore, the courses must be entertaining and interactive.

Students should complete a course evaluation survey after each class. This evaluation will tell you if both the instructor and the materials are effective or if modifications are necessary. Keeping the curriculum *relevant* means ensuring that the classes hit home for the students. The content should be meaningful to the employees, not overly theoretical, and should contain an abundance of real-life examples. Employees should be able to return to their jobs and immediately apply what they've learned.

Structure the employee development system by using a formal curriculum with course descriptions. This will let people know what courses should be taken, and will provide employees with a sense of achievement when they have completed the necessary courses. The best way to accomplish this is to install a training certification system. Develop a separate curriculum for the various generic job categories, such as technical, administrative, and sales. Then, split them into the appropriate levels within the job category (such as technicians, engineers, and managers). Next, challenge the workforce to get certified over time. Honor this accomplishment with a certificate that employees can place in their cubicles or take home.

Since the purpose of the company is not to be a training institution, spread the training out over time and allow employees with equivalent knowledge to get credit for the class. In addition to maintaining a formal certification program, you will need to set up a system to track training and get feedback. Once a quarter, each employee and the manager should be sent a tracking sheet that lists the classes the employee has completed toward certification. In addition, the manager can use these tracking and feedback sheets as a reference when filling out the employee's annual performance appraisal.

The Power of Organizational Development Activities

The employee development system must also focus on developing groups or teams of people. Organizational Development provides services in areas such as team building, style coaching, facilitation, problem solving, visioning, focus groups, and surveys. The OD personnel play a vital role in the *Aggregate System*. They can assist in such things as enhancing your various teams' productivity, running focus groups to identify employee issues, coaching key personnel, assessing the employees' job satisfaction, and monitoring the overall health of the culture.

In general, Human Resources representatives should make better use of the OD people. Many issues employees bring to Human Resources are more effectively resolved when addressed by OD personnel. For example, let's say a supervisor's management style is having a negative impact on his or her staff. Our first course of action would be to improve the situation by assigning an OD professional to work with the manager on his or her management style. If progress turned out to be limited, we would utilize some of the formal processes available to Human Resources to modify the manager's behavior, such as written warnings or performance improvement plans. The power of individual coaching and finding mentors within the organization will be the wave of the future. Therefore, training must become more individualized and real-time oriented.

The Employee Advancement System

The purpose of the advancement system is to ensure that the appropriate people are either promoted or assigned to positions with greater responsibilities. This sounds simple enough. However, all too often, people not really suited for a promotion are given the added responsibility. We see this happen mostly in the transition from individual contributor to supervisor or manager or from manager to senior manager. The breakdown usually occurs because the recently promoted employee lacks people management, project management, communication, interpersonal, or organizational skills. Another problem arises when the promoted individual isn't flexible and adaptable.

Too often we see promotions where the manager of the person being promoted isn't quite sure if the person will be successful in the new position. Often, the manager of the promoted person feels pressured to promote the individual, or the manager concludes that, given the circumstances, it's the best option.

The criteria used in determining promotions should, in general, be consistent with the selection criteria used in the staffing system. Basically, you want to promote the same kind of person you want to hire. The person being promoted should have values and expectations similar to those of the company. If the company values quality, for example, and the individual being promoted is concerned primarily with the quantity of work produced, trouble is on the horizon.

Rather than hiring an external candidate, promote from within the company whenever possible. The internal person is a known quantity who has already assimilated the culture and knows a lot about the company. Even when you verify references, hiring from outside the company is a gamble. The individual may interview extremely well but may turn out to be a marginal performer. It's important to internal employees that you attempt to provide them with career opportunities before you seek out external candidates.

Another tip: survey the employees to verify that your internal transfer system is operating properly. We've seen two areas that break down. The first is when employees are afraid that their supervisor will be upset, or will hold it against them, that they're looking for a position outside the department. The second is that the releasing supervisor won't allow employees to transfer in a reasonable time frame. To solve the problem of supervisor resentment, you must establish a process where the current supervisor is not notified that the employee is interviewing. Let's face it— if the same employee were interviewing with a competitor, the supervisor would not know about that either. So, keep the process low key and confidential until you're ready to make an offer to the internal candidate. Then get the current supervisor involved. To eliminate this awkwardness, have a formal policy that employees must transfer within four weeks. Your policy should also state that the transfer to the new position within the company must transpire in four weeks or less. If the employee was taking a job at a different company they probably would only give you two weeks' notice.

Career Development and Succession Planning

Let us briefly discuss career development and succession planning as it pertains to the advancement system. The company should establish a career development program, along with a small career development center, for the employees. Our experience is the employees like the fact that the company has a career development program. This should consist of workshops on career planning, documents that show the generic job ladders of various positions, and someone in Human Resources or Training who can help describe career paths and provide counsel.

Succession planning, on the other hand, is more problematic. It's important that you move individuals into positions of greater responsibility. It's also important that you have a good idea of who will take a manager's position if the manager leaves. However, the quandary is that the job market, the operation, and the employee population are so dynamic that, by the time you're ready to promote the successor, everything's changed. There may have been a reorganization to make the position obsolete, perhaps a better candidate was identified, or maybe the person left the firm when a more attractive opportunity surfaced.

Problems can also arise with the successor. The potential successor can fall out of favor or can begin to act as if the position was already granted. This typically turns people off and takes away their hope to obtain the position next. We are not trying to discourage succession planning; we're just articulating some of the concerns and pitfalls associated with the process. One remedy is to identify two or three potential successors out of whom one will be chosen at the appropriate time. The keys are to not overly structure the process and to make it as dynamic as is practical. The more senior the position, the greater the expectation that a successor should be waiting in the wings. So, at the executive level, potential successors must be identified and ready for the challenge if and when the opportunity materializes.

18

Performance Appraisals

MANAGERS CAN EVALUATE their employees' performance using a variety of methods. This chapter will focus on the most well-known and widely utilized assessment measure, the annual employee performance appraisal. The performance appraisal is a powerful tool because it serves both as an assessment tool and a development instrument. It provides a permanent record of employees' performance throughout their tenure with the enterprise. Numerous companies fail to exploit the chief attribute of performance appraisals: their ability to support the alignment of the enterprise. Performance appraisals, if designed properly, are much more than a formal review of one's performance. They're a vehicle to ensure employees are reinforced to, and rewarded for, practicing the company's values, helping it attain its strategic formula. Therefore, appraisals play a critical role in the formation and success of the *Aggregate System*.

Strategic Formula
↓
Company's Values
↓
Policies & Procedures
↓
Management Practices
↓
Human Systems
Performance Appraisals
↓
Employee Practices

Performance Appraisal Criteria

The performance appraisal criteria specify the areas in which employees will be assessed. They include the quality and quantity of work, customer satisfaction, innovations, and improvements to the operation. The criteria for assessing employees' performance must be based on the company's values to ensure alignment within the *Aggregate System*. It's key that the performance appraisal utilize the same criteria for all employees. Clearly, based on the employee's job responsibilities, the specific standards for each job will vary substantially. However, the criteria won't vary. For example, all employees will be judged on the quality of their work. The standards used to evaluate the quality of the work completed by a Vice President are not relevant to those used for engineers. What's important, though, is that the company values quality and therefore everyone's work is assessed against this criterion.

Supervisors and managers must be evaluated against additional criteria specific to their managerial responsibilities. These criteria can include employee communication, monitoring, development, and empowerment. The criteria should shape the desired style of management.

What Is Job Performance?

At first glance, evaluating someone's job performance seems straightforward. However, each evaluator may apply a different set of criteria and specific standards based on personal values and expectations. Some managers may evaluate the employee's performance independent of the environment in which the work was completed. Other managers may evaluate the performance in the context of the quality of supervision, tools provided, and training the employee received.

Figure 18.1 illustrates the components that constitute employee performance. Employees' job performance is a result of their behavioral attributes and the environment in which they work. *Behavioral attributes* include expertise, adaptability, rate of improvement, commitment, and the effort employees expend. The *work environment* represents the company's

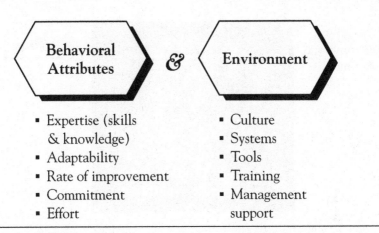

FIGURE 18.1: Components that Constitute Employee Performance

culture, systems, and policies. It also includes the degree of supportive management, tools, and training that individuals receive. Employees' performance can be fairly assessed only when the manager accounts for all these environmental factors.

Employee actions yield varying degrees of value to the company. *Realized value* is the true value a company gains as a result of an employee's accomplishments. Some actions may add great value and others very little, even though the employee is a diligent worker. On occasion an employee may work hard but not solve the problem at hand, while on a different occasion, the employee may have obtained outstanding results with minimal effort. If we redefine employee actions as behaviors, we can conclude that there's a cost associated with every behavior. The ultimate objective is to achieve the desired accomplishment with the fewest behaviors possible. Therefore, we obtain the objective at the lowest cost. This yields maximum effectiveness and efficiency, as illustrated in Figure 18.2.

The Science of Performance Appraisals

When a company creates a performance appraisal designed to align employees with its strategic formula and values, the process begins by specify-

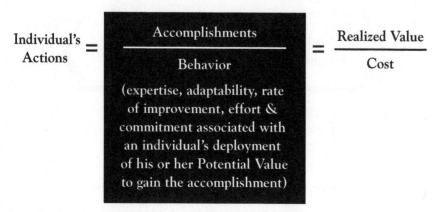

$$\text{Individual's Actions} = \frac{\text{Accomplishments}}{\text{Behavior}} = \frac{\text{Realized Value}}{\text{Cost}}$$

(expertise, adaptability, rate of improvement, effort & commitment associated with an individual's deployment of his or her Potential Value to gain the accomplishment)

*In the context of the **environmental** factors: culture, systems, tools, training, & management support provided*

FIGURE 18.2: Assessing Employee Performance

ing the input and output variables associated with obtaining realized value. Behavioral attributes are the input variables that influence the output variable, the accomplishment, or realized value. As mentioned in Chapter 6, you can change the output variable only by changing the input variables. Therefore, if you want to achieve more, you need to enhance the employees' behavioral attributes.

Figure 18.3 reflects how the employees' behavioral attributes represent their potential to add tangible value to the enterprise. The strength of each specific attribute increases the probability that the employees' performance will produce accomplishments that add value to the enterprise. The accomplishments produced by employees should be viewed as realized value—such as the amount of work the employee produced, the quality of that work, the employee's ability to satisfy the customer (internal or external), and any improvements the employee has made to the operation.

Realized value represents accomplishments that in fact add value to the operation. It's critical to make the distinction between potential and realized value, because in the final analysis, the company runs and improves based on realized value. For instance, just because an employee has

Potential Value to Company **Employee Development** (Input Variables)	**Realized Value to Company** **Primary Assessment Criteria** (Output Variables)
Measurements of an individual's behavioral attributes (abilities & efforts) leading to accomplishments when properly executed:	**Measurements of accomplishments that add actual value to the operation (final results of an employee's work):**

Measurements of an individual's behavioral attributes (abilities & efforts) leading to accomplishments when properly executed:

- Technical & Job Knowledge
- Attention to Detail
- Creativity & Resourcefulness
- Decision Making & Judgment
- Flexibility, Adaptability, & Versatility
- Communication & Documentation
- Planning & Organizing
- Administrative
- Managing Programs, Meetings, & Time
- Managing Change
- Leadership & Role Modeling
- Attitude
- Selling, Persuasiveness, & Negotiating
- Interacting with Others (Interpersonal)
- Analytical & Problem Solving
- Initiative, Motivation, & Perseverance
- Work Habits & Working under Stress
- Meeting Commitments & Follow-through
- Trustworthiness
- Dependability & Attendance
- Presentations
- Visioning & Strategic Thinking
- Work Load Capability
- Profit & Loss Sensitivity
- Delegating
- Self-development
- Risk Taking
- Teamwork

Measurements of accomplishments that add actual value to the operation (final results of an employee's work):

Quality of Work
- Accuracy
- Comprehensiveness
- Etc.

Customer Satisfaction (Internal or External)
- Meeting Commitments
- Responsiveness
- Customer Relations
- Etc.

Quantity of Work
- Amount of Achievements
- Complexity
- Conditions Overcome
- Etc.

Improvements to Operation/Innovations
- People
- Systems
- Methods
- Products & Services
- Cost Structure
- Etc.

Teamwork

FIGURE 18.3: Potential Value vs. Realized Value: Keeping Your Input and Output Variables Straight

incredible technical knowledge doesn't mean that this employee can apply that knowledge to produce realized value. We've seen brilliant individuals who have difficulty producing results due to their poor communication skills, inability to adapt, inadequate interpersonal skills, lack of follow-through, poor judgment, or insufficient effort.

Confusing Potential and Realized Value

Companies frequently fail to maintain the distinction between behavioral attributes (potential value) and accomplishments (realized value) when designing performance appraisals. We've seen companies whose primary measurement is the employee's potential value. They place minimal emphasis on realized value. Hence, they fail to assess the most important thing: what value the employee actually added to the operation. For example, if the employee enhanced his or her technical skills, but this did not improve that employee's contributions to the company, then only individual potential value increased; the company's value did not.

Behavioral attributes drive the obtainment of accomplishments, so they also need to be assessed. A separate section of the appraisal must be dedicated to assessing the employee's behavioral attributes. Because additional gains in realized value are achieved only by developing or strengthening one or more of the employee's behavioral attributes, this second section of the appraisal focuses on employee development. For example, if you want to improve the quality of the employee's work, you may want to advise the employee to enhance his or her decision-making abilities, attention to detail, follow-through, or project management skills. This section should constitute a significant portion of the appraisal.

In some circumstances it's advantageous to treat a specific behavioral attribute as if it represents realized value. This is appropriate when the attribute is vital to the success of the company. For example, as shown in Figure 18.3, teamwork was incorporated into the primary criteria because the company wanted to ensure accomplishments were obtained through teamwork. However, this should be done sparingly or you'll end up watering down the importance of realized value.

Components of Performance Appraisals

Performance appraisals need to strike a balance between providing the employee with an in-depth assessment and setting out a development plan to facilitate further growth. It should not be designed so it's too burdensome for managers to write. Our approach for finding this balance lies in utilizing verbal discussions, rather than text, for portions of the appraisal. For example, the appraisal can specify a comprehensive list of the generic employee behavioral attributes. Managers can then efficiently review their assessment of the employee's degree of mastery of each attribute. The appraisal can be designed so that each behavioral attribute has an adjoining box that can be checked to indicate if the attribute is a strength, an area for further development, or not applicable to the employee's current job. This will serve as documentation of the conversation.

Performance appraisals should consist of the following components:

- The evaluation period
- The overall rating
- A summary of responsibilities or job assignment
- A summary of achievements
- An assessment of how the employee performed based on the company's criteria against which all employees are evaluated
- Additional performance criteria specifically for managers
- Developmental areas consisting of both a written summary of the manager's assessment and a comprehensive list of generic behavioral attributes for further verbal discussion
- Manager's feedback on the employee's career goals

Employee Self-Assessment

The purpose of an employee self-assessment is to ensure that the employee becomes involved in the appraisal process. It also provides managers with insight into how employees assess themselves and the environmental factors they think affected their performance.

Since the self-assessment allows employees to provide input before the manager writes the appraisal, it highlights discrepancies between the manager's assessment and the employee's assessment. Let's say, for example, that as an employee's manager, you know that he has demonstrated poor judgment several times. In reading his self-assessment, you're astonished that he touts good judgment as his best strength. However, being conscious of this disconnect affords you some time to reevaluate your conclusions, or to determine a strategy for addressing this with the employee.

Self-assessment should consist of the following components:

- The period covered
- The job assignments
- A summary of achievements and their significance
- A summary of missed goals and their significance
- The employee's strengths (e.g., provide a comprehensive list of generic behavioral attributes for the employees to select from)
- The employee's areas for further development
- Any significant environmental factors influencing the employee's performance
- The employee's career goals

Why Managers Don't Write Good Performance Appraisals

The two things managers hate the most is being critical of an employee in a one-on-one situation and terminating an employee. Telling employees the honest truth about them as we see it is uncomfortable for most of us. We do not like to criticize people to their faces, unless we're really angry with them. Hence, when writing and delivering appraisals, managers typically soften their legitimate criticism of employees. This softening robs employees of honest feedback and decreases their accountability.

Managers often dedicate insufficient time to writing a comprehensive, well-thought-out appraisal. The manager may not clearly describe the areas requiring development or may fail to spell out the development plan. It's not uncommon for the employee to be surprised by issues raised in the appraisal. Either the manager failed to communicate these issues periodically during the year, or the employee failed to register the feedback.

If the appraisal is highly critical, some managers show anger toward the employee when delivering it. This is their way of dealing with their anxiety about having to criticize someone in such a personal manner. Managers can also rush the delivery of the appraisal, making employees feel their hard work is not valued. Some managers don't take the time to read the employee's self-assessment, which becomes apparent to the employee during the delivery of the appraisal. One of the most common mistakes managers make is failing to seek out the input of the employee's customers (internal or external) and coworkers prior to writing the appraisal.

The following are comments we've heard employees make about their managers after receiving a poorly executed performance appraisal. We've asked, "How did your appraisal go?" They replied:

- "I don't know what's worse—that he wrote practically nothing or that he delivered it in seven minutes!"
- "He obviously has no idea what I do!"
- "Well, that's the first time I've heard all that stuff!"
- "We never even talked about my performance!"
- "Boy, he sure seemed angry when he delivered my performance appraisal!"
- "Man, he thinks I'm doing badly, but he provided no direction to make things better!"
- "I know I can improve, but why did he have to say it like that!"
- "She said everything is fine, but I know I need to do better and still grow! I wish she would just tell me the truth."
- "I'm not sure. It's five months late and I still haven't received it!"
- "She slid it under my door this year!"

Associating Rewards with Performance

Since rewards play a significant role in shaping behavior, it's important that salary merit increases, promotions, and stock options accompany the performance appraisal. By design, you want to link performance with rewards. It also gives the whole process of an annual assessment more clout. Create a healthy ritual for employees and managers to sit down once a year to communicate, and reward employees for their hard work.

Measuring and Improving the Distribution of Performers

By its very nature, attempting to ascertain the merit of an individual's performance, or that of the entire employee population, is problematic. The questions that arise are, "How do we account for, or correct, the varying expectations, criteria, and standards used among our supervisors?" and "How do we know if our 'average performer' is superior to the average performer of our competitors?" You cannot provide a direct answer to unknown or varying conditions. Therefore, relative rather than absolute measures are required. Norm reference measures and fixed distributions can help you negate the lack of absolute criteria.

The two basic approaches to measuring or assessing individuals are criterion and norm reference measures. *Criterion* reference measures are utilized when the true criteria are known. For example, can a person correctly operate a particular piece of equipment, name the capital of each state, or run the mile in under eight minutes? This represents the college class you attended where if all students got the answers correct, they all received an A grade. Since we can't ascertain the abilities and performance of a true average performer, this approach is not applicable. If you told all supervisors, "If your employees meet your expectations and criteria they can all receive the highest rating," the process would soon spin out of control. Seventy percent of the employees would be rated outstanding.

Therefore, when ranking and rating employees, companies need to utilize *norm* reference measures. These are measures of how an individual performs relative to other individuals. In college, we knew this as grading on a curve. Individuals are assessed based on a normal distribution. For example, the top 20% of performers are rated outstanding, 75% are successful, and 5% need improvement. When you enforce this type of distribution and allow no exceptions, it's referred to as a fixed distribution.

This approach is used so the company's theoretical average performer

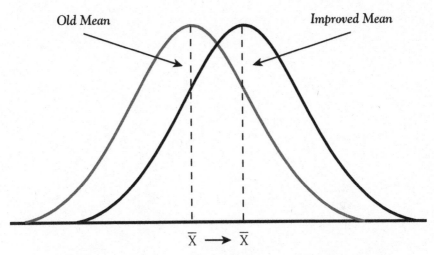

Goal: *Move up the average overall performance by ensuring all employees continuously enchance their performance and by making the lowest performers improve or forcing them to leave the orginization*

FIGURE 18.4: Goal of Fixed Distribution: Improving the Average (Mean)

will systematically get stronger. This is important because it is difficult to know at what level your competitors' average performer is performing. If you knew this, you could use a criterion reference measure to evaluate your employees.

The fixed distribution can also help improve the relative performance of your average performer and identify your lower performers. If you want to continually increase the performance of your mean or average performer (over the employee population) you force the bottom of the distribution, let's say the bottom 5%, to automatically be placed on a formal corrective action plan. Figure 18.4 illustrates that enforcement of the distribution can raise the overall mean or average performer in a company. Figure 18.5 shows how this same approach will eventually result in your company surpassing your competitors.

However, strict adherence to a fixed distribution that forces the bottom performers to automatically be placed on a formal performance improvement plan can lead to undesirable consequences. It can create ill will

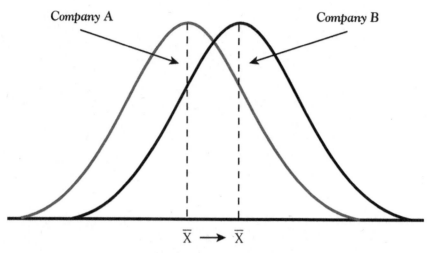

Average (Mean) Overall Performer

Goal: Make your average overall performer stronger than your competitors'
by improving the performance of all employees and by making the
lowest performers improve or forcing them to leave the orginization

Figure 18.5: Stirctly Enforcing Fixed Distributions to Obtain Superior Employee
Performance as Compared to Competitors

with both your supervisors and employees if the percentage is too high. We
prefer to address the lower performers based on the judgment of the functional manager and Human Resources representative. We do not want to
build in a system that may negatively affect the desired culture of the company. A little sound judgment and common sense will allow you to find the
correct balance in addressing the lower performers.

Employee Practices and Assessing the Culture

IN A VALUES-BASED, highly empowered, continuous-improvement culture, the employees truly become the magic ingredient for optimizing the *Aggregate System*. All improvements stem from the efforts of employees. For example, a new piece of equipment to increase manufacturing's efficiency doesn't select and install itself. A novel approach to solving a persistent quality issue comes from an individual or team driven to find a solution. Technology is a critical tool for improving most operations—automation and the computerization of the business processes have yielded extraordinary benefits. However, we can't lose sight that people are at the heart of all great enterprises.

The importance of feedback from the customer and the indicators placed to measure the status of the business' performance and its internal processes is obvious. Less apparent are the tremendous benefits associated with obtaining feedback from the entire employee population. Periodically surveying employees can help you gain insight into the health of the company's culture, the percentage of time the company's values are practiced, the perception of management, and the employees' job satisfaction. It reveals what the employees like about the company and what needs improvement. Further, it reinforces that senior management values the employees' input and involvement.

Experience the Magic

The entire *Aggregate System* is simply a systematic approach to unleash the employees' full potential in order to maximize the value they provide the enterprise. When employees are committed and aligned to the company's values and objectives, the results can be astounding. The workforce enhances the firm independent of management's presence. Each day, the workforce engages in countless decisions and actions to improve the company's performance. When this occurs, you'll experience the magic.

Let's say, for example, that the CEO informs the workforce that expenses are too high. Immediately he sees cost savings occurring throughout the enterprise. Without being asked, individuals are stretching their office supplies. Teams are forming to investigate methods for reducing costs. Purchase orders for new PCs have practically ceased. This is occurring without the CEO having to repeatedly harp on the organization to cut costs. Employees have learned to readily practice the company's values of frugality and profits. So on their own volition they're acting in accordance with the company's values.

Employee Empowerment

If employees don't feel empowered, and aren't given an appropriate level of responsibility and authority, most won't develop the hunger to constantly improve the enterprise. One of the primary reasons to empower employees is that the ever-increasing complexity of the business' internal processes has caused the workforce to be extremely specialized. Managers often are no longer experts in all the areas under their supervision. Also, the number and responsibilities of employees are expanding due to the flattening of organizational hierarchies. Thus, managers are increasingly using employees' intellect and abilities to cope with these changing conditions. In addition, the workforce is becoming more educated. Typically, the more

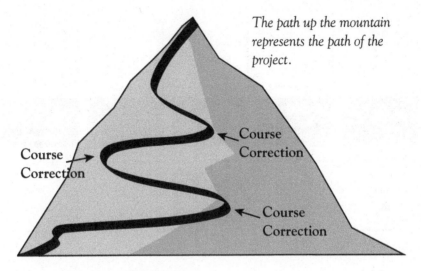

The path up the mountain represents the path of the project.

Course Correction

Course Correction

Course Correction

The manager empowers employees to maximize their task-ownership and enthusiasm.

Figure 19.1: When Coaching, Course Correct; Don't Micromanage

highly educated the workforce, the more freedom they seek in accomplishing assignments.

Employee empowerment requires the manager to act as coach, developer, and facilitator, rather than micromanager. As shown in Figure 19.1, managers should allow employees to define their course of action and provide course correction as appropriate. This is how you enhance the employees' enthusiasm and task-ownership (commitment to take full responsibility in completing the given task). Enthusiasm and task-ownership more than offset the employees' increased learning curve.

If you consistently micromanage the employees' course of action you'll decrease their motivation. Moreover, they will not expand their judgment, expertise, and abilities. It's like that old saying: it's better to teach people to grow food rather than just feeding them.

Figure 19.2 shows an organizational chart that symbolizes management's role in fostering employee empowerment. The chart may seem strange to you because the components of the figure are upside down: the

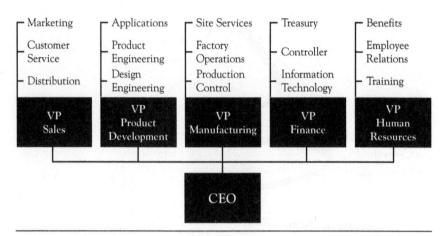

FIGURE 19.2: Abridged Example of an *Upside Down* Organizational Chart

CEO is at the bottom of the chart and the employees are positioned at the top. We recommend that firms draw their organizational charts this way to remind management that their role is to act as coaches, developers, facilitators, and removers of barriers that impede their employees' progress. Further, it serves to remind management that the employees closest to the work are implementing the changes that drive the enterprise's rate of improvement.

Using Figure 19.2, visualize yourself at the bottom of the chart. Consider how you would manage your employees differently if you actually worked for them. Think of the questions that you would ask, how you would ask them, and how those questions would be different than the ones you ask with your current management style. For example, if you act as if you work for your employees, you are more likely to ask, "How can I help you?" instead of "What have you done for me lately?" Which question do you think encourages employees to take initiative, make improvements, or come to you when they need help? The CEO or manager must remove the obstacles in the path of the employees' optimal productivity. This allows the employees to spend their time making improvements rather than trying to guess what the CEO or manager wants to hear.

Empowerment is effective only when it becomes part of the company culture. This requires considerable training to achieve. In most cases, the empowered employees will adopt the expectations and level of aggressiveness of their leader. The leader has to set the example and serve as a role model. The job of the CEO or a manager is not to accumulate and wield power, but to distribute that power wisely throughout the organization, while teaching, guiding, and motivating employees in its use. This principle of employee empowerment is quite simple, yet it is often difficult to implement.

Since power is distributed throughout highly empowered organizations, it is essential to have good communication with the employees. If employees operate with ambiguous expectations or if they lack key information, they will make poor decisions. Remember, often it's not what you say, but how you say it, that motivates and encourages employees. In a highly empowered environment, the traditional, functional power of managers is lessened. Therefore, managers need to become more sophisticated in their ability to sell their ideas and influence employees. In the upside-down chart shown in Figure 19.2, the managers are more likely to treat employees with respect and dignity, listening to their ideas and behaving toward them as they would want to be treated themselves. This is accomplished only when you live and practice the upside-down chart. So don't just draw it, use it.

The 18 Desired Characteristics of Employees

Figure 19.3 shows the 18 desired characteristics of employees. It illustrates that the employees' roles are expanding in scope and complexity. It's difficult to consistently hire employees who possess all 18 characteristics. The *Aggregate System* is designed to overcome this issue. The most critical component in the entire *Aggregate System*, however, remains hiring the right people, individuals who are diligent workers and whose workplace values are aligned with the company's values.

Employee Performance Output Equation

When you're hiring and/or assessing employees' performance relative to that of their peers, it's crucial to clearly understand the total contribution

1. Practices the culture.
2. Achieves the desired results and meets commitments.
3. Produces quality work, takes the job seriously, and displays good work habits.
4. Strives to make improvements to the operation.
5. Seeks to satisfy customers (internal and external).
6. Is bright and has good common sense and technical competence in his/her field.
7. Can handle empowerment and desires to be involved.
8. Works well with others; is a team player with good interpersonal interactions who can work within a consensus approach.
9. Demonstrates good effort, perseverance, and dependability (including attendance).
10. Shows initiative, creativity, and resourcefulness.
11. Has good communication skills.
12. Listens actively and considers others' input and feedback.
13. Has good judgment, is well organized, and operates with limited ego.
14. Is a continuous learner and desires to enhance his/her skills and knowledge.
15. Uses good analytical and problem-solving skills.
16. Shows flexibility and adaptability, and responds well to change.
17. Acts safely, ethically, and honestly.
18. Is frugal (i.e., profit and loss/cost sensitivity).

FIGURE 19.3: The 18 Desired Characteristics of Employees

of the employees. We believe that the traditional view of employees' performance is too restrictive to account for their true output and their effect on other employees. Further, in the *Aggregate System*, employees who continuously improve themselves, who are adaptive and committed, and who positively affect those around them are the superior performers. In the long run, these types of individuals will outperform the traditional hot-shot egoists, whose performance we tend to evaluate independent of their effect on

Employee's Output	=	Expertise (knowledge & skills)	+	Rate of Improvement & Adaptability	×	Contribution to the Environment		×	Effort & Commitment
		(0 to 10)		*(0 to 1)*		*(–10 to +10)*			*(0 to 1)*

Hot Shot Egoist:

$$8.1 = (\quad 9 \quad + (\quad 0.1 \quad \times \quad -9 \quad)) \times \quad 1.0$$

Continuously Improving Team Player:

$$15.1 = (\quad 7 \quad + (\quad 0.9 \quad \times \quad +9 \quad)) \times \quad 1.0$$

Source: Microchip Technology

FIGURE 19.4: Employee Performance Output Equation: Optimizing Employee Performance

the entire team. Figure 19.4, the employee performance output equation, illustrates this premise.

Figure 19.4 begins by showing how the employees' performance depends on their prior expertise (i.e., knowledge and skills). We grade these aspects on a scale of 0 to 10. The employees' output also depends on their rate of improvement and their ability to adapt (scale of 0 to 1), multiplied by the contribution to the environment (scale of –10 to +10). The whole equation is further multiplied by their effort and commitment (scale of 0 to 1). In the case of an employee who considers him- or herself a hot-shot egoist, we give him or her 9 for his expertise. However, he or she tends to have little ability to improve or adapt, and he or she often contributes negatively to the environment. Thus, his or her net score is 8.1. Since the hotshot egoist thinks that he or she walks on water, he or she is a poor team player, upsets others, does not take direction well, and tends to bring the whole team down with his or her self-centered, egotistical style. But the employee still believes that he or she delivers high output because of his or her expertise.

Figure 19.4 also shows the score of an employee who is a continuously improving team player. This individual receives a 7 for expertise. But he or she shows a high rate of improvement and ability to adapt. Further, he or she contributes positively to his or her teammates and the environment, so he or she receives a high score in these areas. In our example, he or she receives a performance output score of 15.1. This equation demonstrates that a group of hard-working, continuously improving team players can receive twice the output compared to a bunch of hot-shot egoists who can't work together, divide the team, and bring the environment down.

Based on the examples given in Figure 19.4, you can clearly see that companies and managers who measure the output of employees based solely on the employees' expertise, while ignoring the other components specified in the equation, are limiting the firm's capabilities. In this brutally competitive global environment, no company can afford to do this.

Intrinsic Reinforcement

Values-based cultures can produce a greater degree of intrinsic reinforcement than rules-based cultures. Intrinsic reinforcers are behaviors that are not driven from external reinforcers (e.g., money, recognition), but rather stem from an internal form of reinforcement. It's great when you hear your son in college say, "Dad, I'm not just sitting in class memorizing the words on the chalkboard anymore. I've realized that I want to learn the information because I enjoy learning new things. You know, earlier on I was attending college because that's what we all do. Now I'm attending college because I like learning the subjects. And I'm going to apply what I've learned after graduation."

You say goodbye, hang up the phone, and think, "Wow, he finally got it." The act of learning itself became the intrinsic motivator that is driving his studying rather than the consequences of poor grades or not graduating. This will significantly increase his probability of graduating and retaining the knowledge long term.

Empowering employees to take increased ownership for completing their work and improving their area of responsibility can provide employees with a sense of accomplishment that acts as a form of intrinsic reinforcement.

Formally Assessing and Enhancing the Culture

It's essential that you formally assess the culture from time to time. During the first few years, conduct a formal assessment at least annually. Businesses typically measure what's important to their success. If you feel that the health and effectiveness of the culture are key aspects of the firm's formula for success, you must measure them. Assessing the culture provides insight into what's working well and what areas require more effort from management.

Management is frequently inaccurate in its qualitative assessment of how the employees perceive the culture and management. Management commonly overestimates the health of the culture and the employees' perception of it. Further, some management teams either don't care about employee input or are afraid of what they might hear. However, it's always advantageous to know your employees' perceptions. Managing with your head in the sand never produces a world-class culture.

Don't be hesitant to share the results of the formal assessment with employees. Reviewing the results reinforces that the health and effectiveness of the culture are important. Doing so shows the employees that their input is appreciated. Moreover, it demonstrates management's sincere interest in its people. It demonstrates that the organization is all one team striving to improve everything, including the culture and management itself. Share the overall findings with the employees. However, avoid going into great detail, since you don't want to lose the focus on the larger issues. (Refer back to Figures 1.7 and 1.8 to see the results of a Microchip formal assessment.)

When the survey uncovers issues, construct a viable strategy to improve things. The survey will typically reveal specific items that require management's attention. For example, the employees frequently want increased pay. They may also want expanded health benefits at a reduced cost. Sometimes the company can accommodate these requests and sometimes it can't. Deal with these issues in a straightforward manner. Tell the employees you understand their concerns but the company can't afford to increase costs at this time. Then focus on the areas that can be improved with minimal costs.

It often doesn't cost much to rectify a considerable portion of the employees' negative feedback. Moreover, don't forget that much of the feedback will pertain to values not directly related to employees. You'll gather feedback on how the employees feel the firm is performing in the areas of quality, customer service, profitability, safety, communication, continuous improvement, and so on. This feedback provides invaluable insight for management and is an essential element of creating a self-perpetuating improvement system.

The Actual Assessment

There are many avenues for assessing how the company practices its values, including focus groups, luncheons, suggestion boxes, and one-on-one meetings with employees. The single most effective method is an anonymous survey of the entire employee population. Construct an evaluation form that covers the areas suggested here and any others that you want to examine.

On the evaluation form, employees must indicate their work location, years of service, job classification (e.g., technical manager, administrative manager, engineer, administrator, technician, operator/factory worker), and shift. Have the employees indicate the percentage of time the company practices each of its stated values. Have them rate their job satisfaction and what percentage of the time their immediate manager (no names allowed) practices the company's values. Ask the employees what things they like best about the company and what needs improvement. These are open-ended questions that you'll have to subjectively categorize (e.g., pay, stock options, teamwork, communication, safety).

Break down each of the items being measured into the following groupings:

- Entire employee population
- Location

- Years of service
- Job classification
- Shift

Then measure the following items:

- Percentage of time the firm is currently practicing each of its values, expressed in average (mean) scores
- Percentage of time the firm is currently practicing its values, expressed in mode (most frequent score given) scores
- Comparison between the current and historical (previous surveys) percentage of time the firm practices each of its values, expressed in average scores
- Comparison between the current and historical percentage of time the firm practices each of its values, expressed in mode scores
- Percent of time the employee's immediate supervisor is currently practicing the firm's values
- Employees' likes & dislikes, categorized and expressed in percentages
- Employees' job satisfaction, categorized (high, good, so-so, or low) and expressed in percentages

Devise a presentation for senior management based on your analysis of the data. Whenever possible show the data in graphical form. Summarize the findings so that the audience doesn't get lost in the details. To foster discussions with senior management, propose enhancement initiatives that address any issues not covered by the survey. Work with senior management to establish needed initiatives. If the data suggests there are problems in a given area of the firm, further analysis may be warranted. Construct a less-detailed presentation for the employees, and communicate the findings and improvement programs to them.

Summation

THE AGGREGATE SYSTEM represents the next evolutionary step in the study of business management. It shifts the focus from examining the various pieces that constitute the enterprise to comprehending the entire business as a total system, consciously designed to optimize the enterprise's rate of improvement. Its purpose is to maximize the company's rate of improvement by aligning and uniting all elements of the enterprise that influence employee performance. Moreover, the *Aggregate System* approach views company culture and employee performance as systems that must be optimized in order for the firm to realize its improvement potential. Treating culture as a system allows it to be designed, influenced, and controlled.

The key to the success of the *Aggregate System* is its comprehensiveness. It makes certain that every factor that influences employees' performance is understood, aligned, and integrated with all the other influential factors, ensuring the desired culture and business objectives are realized. The *Aggregate System* is founded on the following ten key elements:

1. Inspiring leadership.
2. Continuous-improvement culture.
3. Clear company values.
4. Fully aligned strategies.
5. Employees share in the company's prosperity.

6. Managers serve as role models.
7. Politics, ego, and arrogance not allowed.
8. Systems approach utilized to make improvements.
9. Pursuit of excellence.
10. Engaged board of directors.

Improving all aspects of the enterprise is accomplished by consciously designing it to perpetuate continuous improvement. It involves training, equipping, empowering, and requiring all employees to improve their areas of responsibility. Since employees play a role in all improvements, the secret is to comprehend and effectively manage all the factors that influence job performance to ensure employees strive for excellence. This is accomplished through the use of the *Aggregate System*, in which the company is consciously designed around a core set of values in an attempt to achieve its strategic formula. The company's policies, management practices, and the human systems that influence employees must be aligned and integrated to the values. These human systems encompass how the company organizes, staffs, communicates, assesses, recognizes, compensates, develops, and advances individuals. By consciously designing and managing the totality of factors influencing employees' behavior and performance, you yield exceptional performance from the average employee.

The *Aggregate System* is not just a theoretical or academic exercise. It was employed in the turnaround of Microchip Technology, Inc. Microchip exemplifies the power of the *Aggregate System* at work. The company went from being a struggling company on the verge of liquidation to becoming one of the top-performing semiconductor firms in the industry. This represented a complete and remarkable turnaround in performance. Microchip's success was a result of its ability to sustain an optimum rate of continuous improvement.

The use of the *Aggregate System* is not limited to the semiconductor industry. When implemented correctly, it can be applied to any business. The key is to convert your desire to improve the enterprise into the successful application of the *Aggregate System*. We're confident that using the *Aggregate System* in your firm will yield extraordinary results.

Index

About the Authors

Before retiring in 2004, **Michael J. Jones** was vice president of human re-sources for Microchip Technology Inc. Michael was one of the primary ar-chitects of Microchip's extremely successful company culture. A graduate of California State University, Chico, he holds a Master of Arts degree from the College of Communication and Education and a Bachelor of Arts degree in Psychology. In 2001, he received one of the university's highest honors, Distinguished Alumni, awarded to recognize the most talented and successful alumni. Before joining Microchip, Michael worked for Intel Corporation. He has also served on the board of directors for various com-munity service organizations. Michael authored the children's book *Travis Loses His Way: Adventures That Teach Strong Values*, and wrote and pro-duced two albums, *Beginning Again* and *Chasing Life*.

Steve Sanghi is the president, CEO, and chairman of the board of direc-tors of Microchip Technology Inc. Under his leadership, Microchip earned the distinction of being the top IPO of 1993. Steve holds a Master of Science degree in Electrical and Computer Engineering from the Univer-sity of Massachusetts and a Bachelor of Science degree in Electronics and Communication from Punjab University, India. In June 1995, he received an Arizona Entrepreneur of the Year Award and was a finalist in the Na-tional Turnaround Entrepreneur of the Year category. Before joining Microchip, he was vice president of operations at Waferscale Integration, Inc. Prior to this he was employed by Intel Corporation as general manager of programmable memory operation. Steve co-chairs the State of Arizona Governor's Council of Innovation and Technology, and is a member of the board of trustees of Kettering University, in Flint, Michigan.